THE COMPLETE BOOK OF

Cake Decorating
with Sugarpaste

THE COMPLETE BOOK OF

Cake Decorating with Sugarpaste

Sylvia Coward

NH

NEW
HOLLAND

ACKNOWLEDGEMENTS

My thanks to my daughter, Shelley, who designed the wheelbarrow on page 109 and the dartboard on page 133, to Joan Dymond who created the wishing well on page 77, and to Gail English for her time and assistance in baking and testing the biscuit recipes.

It is with great pride that I acknowledge the contributions made by the following pupils who, under my guidance and supervision, executed my designs to create some of the cakes featured in this book.

Rita Bothma	pages 60 and 78
Shirley Brooks	pages 66, 80 and 106
Jackie Coetzee	pages 82, 94, 116 and 126
Mariette de Haan	pages 70, 74, 86 and 90
Joan Dymond	pages 58, 68, 92 and 108
Gail English	pages 62 and 72
Colleen O'Leary	pages 64 and 76

All cake decorating tools, equipment, supplies and special ingredients by courtesy of THE SUGAR ART SHOP, Edenvale.

New Holland Press
37 Connaught Street
London W2 2A7
United Kingdom

First published in the United Kingdom 1987
Second impression 1988

Copyright © text and photography
Sylvia Coward

Designed by Jennie Hoare
Edited by Linda de Villiers
Typeset by McManus Bros (Pty) Ltd
Illustrated by Gina Daniel
Photography by Tim Frowd AIP and Hilda Kwan
Reproduction by Hirt & Carter (Pty) Ltd
Printed and bounded by Tien Wah Press (Pte) Ltd,
Singapore

ISBN 1 85368 000 1

Contents

*This book is dedicated to all cake decorators —
amateurs and professionals alike — who use their
artistic talents and inclinations to make every special
occasion one to remember.*

*Because the cakes featured here not only look good, but taste
good as well, basic recipes for cakes and icing have been
provided. The fruit cake recipe is one I have used most
successfully for many years for wedding and other special
occasion cakes.*

*As an art form, cake decorating and sugarcraft necessitate
the inclusion of a section on the use of colour as well as the
various tools and accessories required to create these designs.
Unless otherwise stated, I have used Bekenal tubes to pipe the
designs and techniques used in this book.*

*Full colour, step-by-step photographs illustrate clearly the
different decorating techniques of lace work, embroidery and
extension work to name just a few, as well as how to pipe and
mould flowers.*

*Piping Jelly, Cocoa Painting and Wafer Painting, three simple
yet effective techniques, are included together with a variety of
interesting and delightful Easter egg and miniature cake
designs.*

*Included at the back of the book are black and white patterns
so that each cake design can be duplicated.*

*I hope this collection of wedding, Christmas, birthday,
christening, engagement, and other special occasion cakes will
delight and inspire every sugar artist.*

Sylvia Coward

Part One

Tools & Equipment

There are certain basic tools, equipment and special ingredients which are essential for doing the various cake decorating techniques but numerous items can be added for the creation of different effects. The equipment shown here is by no means all that is available but generally covers items used for the cakes and designs featured in this book.

Although it is an advantage to have all the right tools and equipment available, you may not always have access to them. You may, therefore, find items around the house which can be used most successfully.

Anger tool: This is a most useful tool which has many uses including hollowing small flowers.

Ball tools: Various sizes of ball tools are used for modelling and moulding flowers and figures.

Brushes: A selection of good quality paintbrushes in various sizes is essential for creating special effects.

Cocoa butter: This is mixed with cocoa powder and used in the *Cocoa Painting* technique described on page 48.

Container for egg white: A new and unused nail polish bottle and brush is most suitable for storing and applying egg white.

Crimpers: Available in a wide variety of shapes, these are used to create patterns on cakes by pinching the plastic icing together (see page 37).

Florist and tinned copper fuse wire: Florist or fuse wire is inserted into moulded flowers to facilitate the making up of sprays. The sprays are then attached to the cake with royal icing. The wire stems should never be inserted directly into the cake.

Florist tape: This is usually available in white, brown, light and dark green and is used for taping the wires for moulded flowers.

Flower cutters: Numerous metal and plastic cutters are available for making the different flowers.

Flower formers: These are the various plastic and wooden shapes used in the making of different moulded flowers.

Flower nails: A variety of flower nails is available; the one most commonly used consists of a flat metal or plastic disc on a spike and is used for piped royal icing flowers.

Flower stand/holder: I developed this wooden flower stand to facilitate the drying and storing of small moulded flowers.

Flower or leaf veiners: Rubber or plastic shapes that are pressed onto modelling paste to create veining on flowers and leaves.

Frill rulers: Scalloped cutters of different lengths, these are used for cutting modelling paste or pastillage to create a frilled or scalloped edge.

Gum Arabic: This can be used to glaze flowers to create a porcelain effect as well as to make edible glitter (see page 15).

Gum tragacanth: Available from specialist cake decorating shops and pharmacies, this powder is added to create the modelling paste used for making moulded flowers. It gives elasticity and is a drying agent.

1. Workbox 2. Tape cutter 3. Modelling tools 4. Ball tool 5. Ribbon inserter 6. Anger tool 7. Fuse wire 8. Tullen scissors 9. Tube cleaning brush 10. Tweezers 11. Scissors 12. Florist wire 13. Crimpers 14. Flower nails 15. Stamens 16. Egg whitecontainer 17. Wire cutters 18. Gum Arabic 19. Gum tragacanth 20. Hatpins 21. Marbles

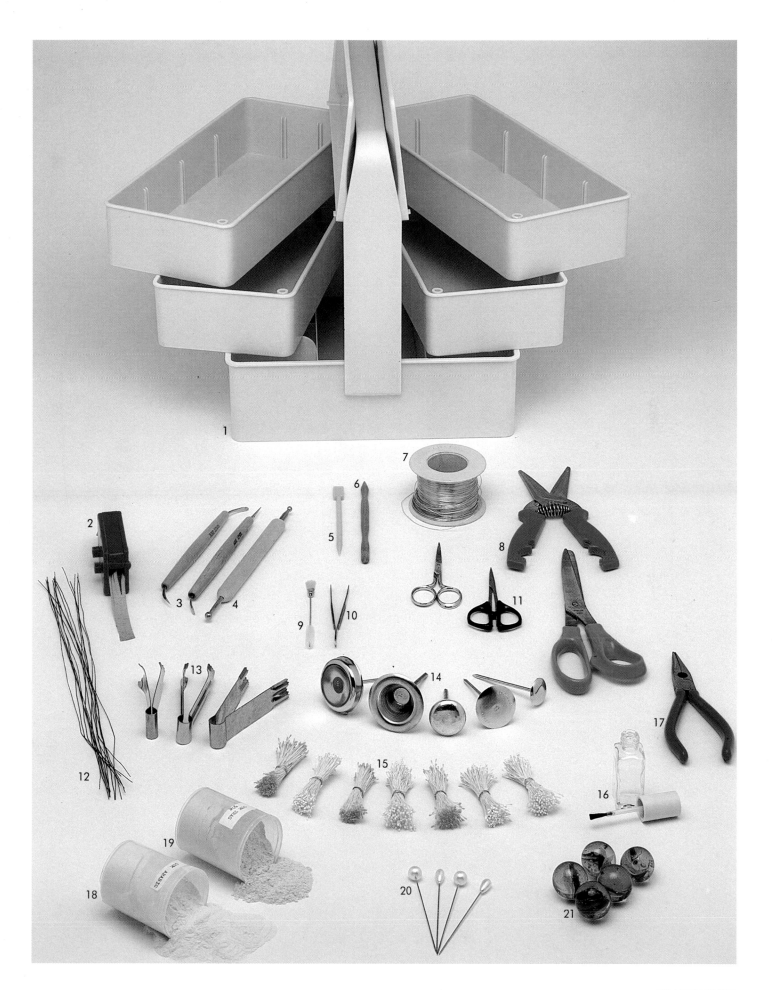

Hobby or icing knife: A small knife is needed for certain types of work to cut modelling paste or pastillage.

Icing bags: For those who prefer not to use paper cones for piping, a nylon icing bag is preferable to the rigid syringe-type.

Lifters: These are made from two pieces of thin board, each measuring 380 x 250 mm, and are used for lifting the marzipan and plastic icing onto the cake.

Manicure tool: Usually found in a manicure set, this tool is used successfully to create the features of the animals found on pages 150-151.

Moulds: Of plastic or plaster, these moulds can be filled with sugar, chocolate or modelling paste. Certain moulds are available for creating figures.

Nozzles: See Tubes.

Painting knife: This is available from art shops and is used for lifting petals, leaves, and so on.

Palette: A small plastic artist's palette with little hollows is useful for mixing colours with water or cornflour and for mixing cocoa powder with cocoa butter in *Cocoa Painting*.

Paper cones: These are made from greaseproof paper and are generally favoured among cake decorators for use with icing tubes. See page 19 for details on how to make paper cones.

Piping jelly: Available from specialist cake decorating shops, piping jelly (page 46) is a fun technique that can be used successfully on most types of icing. It holds its shape but does not set hard. It is piped around the edges of a design and then brushed towards the centre with a small, flat brush.

Ribbon inserter: This is a most useful tool with a flat shape about 10 mm wide on one end which is used to make slits in the icing to allow for the insertion of ribbon. The other end of the tool often has a point for creating a broderie anglaise effect, or a ridged cone for moulding flowers.

Roller: A small chrome or plastic roller is necessary for rolling out modelling paste for moulded flowers.

Rolling board: A wooden board with a melamine or other smooth covering is essential for rolling out modelling paste and pastillage.

Rolling pin: A good quality rolling pin is necessary for rolling out marzipan and plastic icing. Personal preference is the deciding factor. A ribbed roller is very useful for creating various effects on clothes, plaques, and so on.

Scissors: A good pair of small, sharp embroidery scissors is necessary for fine work.

Shears or wire cutters: These are used for cutting wire stems.

Smoothers: Two plastic rectangles used for smoothing the sides and top edges of the marzipan and plastic icing on a cake.

Stamens: The centres of flowers require various stamens, some of which are shown in the relevant photograph.

Straight-edge cutter: Made from extruded acrylic with a sharp cutting edge, this was developed by my daughter to facilitate cutting ribbons or strips of pastillage or modelling paste.

Tape cutter: Used for cutting florist tape into four, making it possible to tape very fine wires smoothly and evenly.

Tube cleaning brush: This looks like a miniature bottle brush and is essential for easy cleaning of tubes after use.

Tubes: Sometimes also referred to as nozzles, icing tubes are available under various brand names. There is no international uniformity in the way in which they are numbered by the various manufacturers, except possibly for certain of the writing tubes. It is a good idea to select the best of each brand according to your purpose. Store the tubes carefully, standing upright, to avoid damage. The most popular tubes and tubes used on the cakes in this book are illustrated on pages 21-23.

Veining and fluting tools: These tools have curved ends and are ideal for figure and flower moulding.

Workbox: Tools and equipment need to be stored neatly and safely and the box shown here is ideal.

1. Turntable 2. Cake board 3. Flower stand 4. Plastic rollers 5. Ribbed roller 6. Rolling pins 7. Plastic moulds 8. Pastry board 9. Hobby knife 10. Table knives 11. Painting knife 12. Craft knife 13. Straight-edge cutters 14. Frill rulers 15. Paper cones 16. Piping jelly 17. Smoothers 18. Leaf veiners 19. Tubes 20. Orchid former

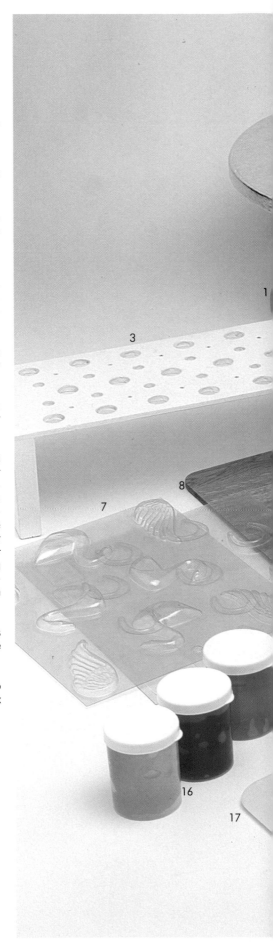

Cake Recipes

Over the years, I have received numerous requests for recipes which I have personally found successful. I have, therefore, included some of my favourites, together with a table of baking times and quantities for different shapes and sizes of cake tins.

FRUIT CAKE

750 g fruit cake mix
125 g dates
125 g cherries
125 g nuts
125 ml brandy
250 g butter or margarine
250 g sugar
6 eggs
5 ml mixed spice
5 ml cinnamon
3 ml ground cloves
5 ml ginger
25 ml syrup
750 ml flour
5 ml bicarbonate of soda

1. Soak the fruit and nuts overnight in brandy.
2. Preheat the oven to 150 °C.
3. Line a 225 mm square cake tin with greaseproof paper.
4. In a large bowl, cream the butter and sugar.
5. Add the eggs, one at a time, mixing well.
6. Add the spices and syrup.
7. Sift in the flour and continue mixing.
8. Add the fruit and nuts.
9. Mix the bicarbonate of soda with 15 ml water and add to the cake mixture. The mixture should be very thick.
10. Pour the mixture into the cake tin and bake for 2¼ hours.
11. When baked, cool the cake on a wire rack for about half an hour to an hour before turning out.

NOTE
1. Should you wish to omit the dates, increase the quantity of fruit cake mix to 875 g.
2. If desired, increase the quantity of mixed spice to 18 ml and omit the cinnamon, cloves and ginger.
3. Baked cakes are approximately 75 mm high.

CHOCOLATE OIL CAKE

Butter icing is most suitable for decorating this cake.

50 ml cocoa
100 ml boiling water
250 ml flour
1 ml salt
10 ml baking powder
4 eggs
200 ml castor sugar
60 ml oil
5 ml vanilla essence
2 ml almond essence

1. Preheat the oven to 200 °C.
2. Grease and line two 175 mm sandwich tins.
3. Blend the cocoa and boiling water and allow to cool.
4. Sift together the flour, salt and baking powder.
5. Beat one egg and three yolks well, then gradually beat in the sugar and continue beating until the mixture is very thick and creamy.
6. Add the cocoa mixture, oil, vanilla and almond essence.
7. Add the flour mixture.
8. Beat the remaining egg whites until stiff peaks form and carefully fold into the cake mixture.
9. Pour the mixture into the prepared tins, tap tins gently to release the air bubbles, and bake for 25 minutes.
10. Turn out onto a wire rack to cool. When cold, fill and ice as desired.

NOTE: This cake freezes perfectly whether decorated or plain.

QUICK SPONGE

Butter or plastic icing can be used most successfully on this cake.

375 ml flour
1 ml salt
10 ml baking powder
185 ml sugar
125 g softened butter or margarine
2 eggs
125 ml milk
5 ml vanilla essence

1. Preheat the oven to 175 °C.
2. Grease and flour a 200 mm round cake tin.
3. Sift the flour, salt, baking powder and sugar into a mixing bowl.

4. Add the butter, eggs, milk and vanilla and beat for 2 to 3 minutes with an electric mixer or for about 5 minutes by hand until well blended.
5. Pour the mixture into the prepared tin and bake for 45 minutes.
6. Turn out onto a wire rack to cool.

NOTE: Bake cup cakes at 200 °C for 10 minutes.

FRUIT, NUT AND CHOCOLATE CAKE

This delicious cake does not need to be iced, but makes a valuable addition to your collection of cake recipes.

250 g butter or margarine
250 ml sugar
4 eggs
500 ml flour
60 ml milk
125 g fruit cake mix
125 g cherries, chopped
125 g pecan nuts, chopped
125 g plain milk chocolate, chopped
3 ml baking powder

1. Preheat the oven to 175 °C.
2. Grease and line a 325 x 100 mm loaf tin.
3. Cream the butter and sugar.
4. Add the eggs one at a time, beating well after each addition.
5. Sift the flour and add to the mixture together with the milk.
6. Add the fruit cake mix, cherries, nuts and chocolate and mix well.
7. Lastly add the baking powder.
8. Pour the mixture into the prepared tin and bake for 1½ hours.
9. Turn out onto a wire rack to cool.

Two recipes to help you use up some of the egg yolks you will have left over after mixing your royal icing.

SWISS TEA DAINTIES

125 g butter
85 mℓ castor sugar
1 egg yolk
60 mℓ ground almonds
375 mℓ flour
3 mℓ baking powder
1 mℓ salt
strawberry or raspberry jam
butter or glacé icing (page 14)
glacé cherries (optional)

1. Preheat the oven to 175 °C and grease a baking tray.
2. Cream the butter and sugar until light and fluffy.
3. Beat in the egg yolk and add the almonds.
4. Sift the flour, baking powder and salt and add to the butter mixture to form a soft dough.
5. Roll out to approximately 5 mm thick and cut into small rounds.
6. Arrange on the baking tray and bake for 10 minutes or until pale gold.
7. Cool on a wire rack and when cold, sandwich two biscuits together with raspberry or strawberry jam, or butter icing.
8. Ice the top with butter or glacé icing.
9. Decorate with half a cherry if desired.

Makes 30

SANDY BISCUITS

250 g sugar
2 eggs
3 egg yolks
300 g flour
5 mℓ baking powder
rind of half a lemon or orange

1. Preheat the oven to 175 °C and grease a baking tray.
2. Beat together the sugar, eggs and egg yolks until 'ribbons' form, about 3 minutes on fast speed.
3. Sift the flour and baking powder and add to the egg mixture together with lemon or orange rind, stirring gently.
4. Pipe long strips or rounds onto the baking tray.
5. Decorate with a raisin and sprinkle with granulated sugar.
6. Let the biscuits rest for at least 1 hour, then bake for 10 to 15 minutes.

Makes 56

APPROXIMATE QUANTITIES OF FRUIT CAKE MIXTURE AND BAKING TIMES

The following quantities of fruit cake mixture and the baking times are approximate for the sizes and shapes of the relevant pans. It is advisable always to test each cake with a cake tester or even a knitting needle to ensure that it is sufficiently baked.

Pan size and shape	Quantity	Baking time
150 mm square	½ x recipe/ 4 cups	2 hours
175 mm square	½ x recipe/ 4 cups	2 hours
200 mm square	¾ x recipe/ 6 cups	2 hours
225 mm square	1 x recipe/ 8 cups	2¼ hours
250 mm square	1½ x recipe/12 cups	2¾ hours
275 mm square	2 x recipe/16 cups	3 hours
300 mm square	2½ x recipe/20 cups	3 hours
325 mm square	3 x recipe/24 cups	3½ hours
350 mm square	3½ x recipe/28 cups	3½ hours
150 mm round	⅜ x recipe/ 3 cups	2 hours
175 mm round	½ x recipe/ 4 cups	2 hours
200 mm round	¾ x recipe/ 6 cups	2 hours
225 mm round	¾ x recipe/ 6 cups	2 hours
250 mm round	1 x recipe/ 8 cups	2¼ hours
275 mm round	1½ x recipe/12 cups	2¾ hours
300 mm round	2 x recipe/16 cups	3 hours
325 mm round	2¼ x recipe/18 cups	3½ hours
350 mm round	2¾ x recipe/22 cups	3½ hours
400 mm round	4 x recipe/32 cups	4½ hours
150 mm hexagonal*	½ x recipe/ 4 cups	2 hours
175 mm hexagonal	½ x recipe/ 4 cups	2 hours
200 mm hexagonal	¾ x recipe/ 6 cups	2 hours
250 mm hexagonal	1½ x recipe/12 cups	2¾ hours
300 mm hexagonal	2¼ x recipe/18 cups	3½ hours
350 mm hexagonal	3 x recipe/24 cups	3½ hours
200 mm petal (scalloped)	½ x recipe/ 4 cups	2 hours
250 mm petal	1 x recipe/ 8 cups	2¼ hours
300 mm petal	1¾ x recipe/14 cups	3 hours
350 mm petal	2½ x recipe/20 cups	3½ hours
200 x 160 mm oval	½ x recipe/ 4 cups	2 hours
250 x 200 mm oval	1 x recipe/ 8 cups	2¼ hours
300 x 250 mm oval	1½ x recipe/12 cups	2¾ hours
250 x 200 mm rectangle	1¼ x recipe/10 cups	2¾ hours
325 x 225 mm rectangle	2 x recipe/16 cups	3 hours
150 x 150 mm heart	⅜ x recipe/ 3 cups	2 hours
225 x 200 mm heart	¾ x recipe/ 6 cups	2 hours
250 x 225 mm heart	1 x recipe/ 8 cups	2¼ hours
300 x 265 mm heart	1½ x recipe/12 cups	2¾ hours
350 x 325 mm heart	2 x recipe/16 cups	3 hours

*NOTE: The measurements given for hexagonal-shaped tins are from side to side.

Icing Recipes

While commercially prepared marzipan, or almond paste, and plastic icing are generally available in large quantities in most areas, they may be unobtainable in country districts. I have, therefore, included the more commonly used recipes necessary to create the designs in this book.

ROYAL ICING

1 egg white
200 g sifted icing sugar
3 drops acetic acid or 1 ml tartaric acid
  or 2 ml lemon juice

1. Place the egg white in a clean glass bowl and beat lightly with a wooden spoon to break up the egg white.
2. Add half the icing sugar, 25 ml at a time, beating thoroughly after each addition.
3. Add the acid or lemon juice.
4. Continue adding icing sugar, 25 ml at a time, until the consistency is like well-beaten cream and holds small peaks.
5. Adjust the consistency for various types of work – a firmer texture is required for piping borders, and a softer consistency for line work.
6. When colouring royal icing, use only a touch of paste colour on the end of a toothpick.

> **NOTE:** Royal icing can be mixed with an electric mixer and will take approximately 5 minutes but about 15 minutes if mixed by hand.

FONDANT ICING

This icing is suitable for coating cakes and for making sweets.

250 g liquid glucose
1 kg sifted icing sugar
10 ml gelatine
50 ml cold water
20 g white vegetable fat

1. Stand the bottle of liquid glucose, with its lid off, in hot water to warm.
2. Set aside approximately 250 ml icing sugar.

3. Soak the gelatine in 50 ml cold water in a small container. Place the container over hot water until the gelatine has completely dissolved.
4. Melt the fat.
5. Make a well in the remaining icing sugar and add the glucose, gelatine and fat.
6. Stir well to combine. Knead the icing and adjust the consistency by either adding some of the reserved icing sugar or egg white until a smooth pliable paste is formed.
7. Store in a plastic bag in an airtight container. Do not place in the refrigerator.

GLACÉ ICING

This icing sets very quickly and must be used while still warm.

15 ml hot water (approx)
flavouring and colouring as required
150 g icing sugar

1. Add water, flavouring and colouring to the icing sugar and stir until a smooth running consistency is obtained.
2. Pour over biscuits, pastry or cakes and allow to set.

> **NOTE:** This quantity will cover a 180 mm cake or 18 cup cakes.

PLASTIC ICING

250 ml granulated sugar
250 g liquid glucose
125 ml water
10 ml gelatine
flavouring and colouring (optional)
1 kg sifted icing sugar
20 g white vegetable fat

1. Place the sugar, glucose and water in a pan and heat gently to dissolve the sugar.
2. Periodically wash down the sides of the saucepan with a wet pastry brush.
3. Bring to the boil and place the lid on for a minute or two so that the steam can wash down the sides of the saucepan.
4. Boil to 106 °C without stirring. This should take approximately 4 minutes.
5. Soak the gelatine in 15 ml cold water.
6. Remove the pan from the stove and when the bubbles subside add the gelatine.
7. Add the flavouring and colouring and half the icing sugar.

8. Sift the remaining icing sugar onto a large wooden or other smooth surface. Make a well in the centre and pour the mixture into it. Add the vegetable fat and mix and knead until a smooth pliable consistency is obtained.
9. Roll out and coat the cake while the icing is still warm.
10. Store in a plastic bag in an airtight container. Do not place in the refrigerator.

> **NOTE:** This icing can be reheated in a casserole in a cool oven at 110 °C.

BUTTER ICING

125 g butter or margarine
500 g icing sugar
5 ml flavouring
small quantity of milk, water or fruit juice

1. Cream butter very well.
2. Add icing sugar gradually.
3. Add flavouring and beat well.
4. Add a little milk, water or fruit juice until a smooth spreading consistency is formed.

MODELLING PASTE 1

This paste improves with age and should be stored in an airtight container.

500 g plastic icing
15 ml gum tragacanth

1. Mix the plastic icing and gum tragacanth together and knead thoroughly.
2. Store in a plastic bag in an airtight container. Do not store in the refrigerator.
3. Break off a piece of paste, dip it into egg white and knead it thoroughly before using.

MODELLING PASTE 2

white margarine or vegetable fat
500 ml sifted icing sugar
25 ml gum tragacanth (purest)
15 ml gelatine
15 ml cold water
15 ml boiling water
1 large egg white
plastic bag

1. Grease a glass mixing bowl with white margarine or vegetable fat, add the icing sugar and place the bowl over hot water.
2. Heat the icing sugar in the bowl.
3. Add the gum tragacanth and stir with

a wooden spoon to heat evenly. Do not let the sugar get moist. Heat to just warmer than blood temperature, then remove the bowl from the water.

4. Prepare the gelatine by sprinkling it onto cold water. Add the boiling water and stand the gelatine in a bowl of hot water to dissolve. Do not place it on the stove as gelatine must never get too hot.

5. Beat the egg white lightly with a fork to break it up.

6. Remove 250 mℓ warm icing sugar and keep it on one side. Add the gelatine and most of the egg white to the icing sugar in the bowl. Stir, mixing quickly and well. Add the remaining icing sugar and beat well.

7. Transfer to a clean, greased bowl and, with clean hands greased with white margarine or vegetable fat, work the paste for 10 to 15 minutes. Add the remaining egg white if the paste seems a little dry or stiff.

8. Shape the paste into a ball, grease the outside with white margarine or vegetable fat and store it in a plastic bag in a sealed container in the refrigerator.

9. Once or twice a week, take out the paste and work it for about five minutes.

SPECIAL MOULDING PASTE FOR FIGURES

500 g plastic icing
10 mℓ gum tragacanth

1. Mix the gum tragacanth into the plastic icing.

2. Allow to mature for at least a week before using. Store this modelling paste in a plastic bag in an airtight container. Do not store it in the refrigerator.

MARZIPAN 1

500 g ground almonds
250 g icing sugar
250 g castor sugar
10 mℓ brandy
8 egg yolks

1. Mix all the dry ingredients together.

2. Add the brandy and sufficient egg yolk to make a paste. Do not knead too much as the marzipan will become oily.

3. Use immediately.

MARZIPAN 2

500 g sugar
250 mℓ water
1 mℓ cream of tartar
125 g ground almonds
1 egg, beaten
5 mℓ ratafia or almond essence

1. Dissolve the sugar in the water over low heat.

2. Do not allow it to boil until the sugar has completely dissolved. Wash down the

sides of the saucepan with a wet pastry brush.

3. Allow the mixture to boil to 120 °C without stirring.

4. Remove it from the heat and allow it to cool for exactly 20 minutes.

5. Add cream of tartar, almonds, egg and essence and beat with a wooden spoon until thick and creamy. Leave to cool.

6. Place the marzipan on a board and knead until smooth.

7. Use immediately.

PASTILLAGE

250 mℓ royal icing
5 mℓ gum tragacanth
dry, sifted icing sugar

1. Mix together the royal icing and gum tragacanth.

2. Add icing sugar until you have a pliable dough that is no longer sticky.

3. Roll out on a piece of glass or board lightly dusted with cornflour and cut out the desired shapes.

4. Keep turning the shapes every few hours until evenly and thoroughly dry.

NOTE: Pastillage is better used immediately, but can be stored in a plastic bag in an airtight container for a few hours.

GUM ARABIC GLAZE

Hot water
Gum Arabic

Mix together thoroughly sufficient quantities of both to form a painting consistency. Paint onto completed moulded flowers and leaves to create a porcelain effect.

EDIBLE GLITTER

50 mℓ hot water
25 g gum Arabic

1. Pour water into a bowl and sprinkle gum Arabic over. Stand the bowl in hot water, stirring gently to dissolve.

2. Strain mixture through a piece of nylon.

3. Brush mixture onto a clean baking tray or glass surface and place in a warm oven (140 °C) until dry.

4. Brush or scrape the dry glitter off the tray and crush it into fine flakes. Store the glitter in an airtight jar.

5. Glitter may be coloured by adding colouring to the water when mixing.

Covering a Cake

The preparation of a cake prior to icing is an essential part of cake decorating. The marzipan seals the fruit cake and prevents it from staining the icing, and together the marzipan and icing form the smooth medium onto which you will pipe or mould your designs. A good base covering will make the final product look so much more professional.

> **NOTE:** Approximately 1 kg each of plastic icing and marzipan is required to cover a 250 mm cake.

1. Place the fruit cake upside down on the cake board. (If the cake has risen to a hump or if it is uneven, trim it until it is level.) Knead the marzipan (page 15) until it is soft and pliable and place it in a plastic bag to prevent it drying out. Roll a thin 'sausage' of marzipan and fill any gaps between the cake and the board and any holes in the cake itself. Smooth over these and around the base of the cake with a knife until the whole surface is even.

2. Measure the distance over the cake with a length of string, starting at the base, then up one side of the cake, across the top and down to the board on the other side. Knot the string to mark the correct length.

3. Bring some smooth apricot jam to a full boil. Spread the hot jam very thinly over the top and sides of the cake.

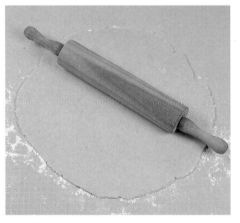

4. Sprinkle dry icing sugar onto a table top or pastry board. Roll out the marzipan until it is about 5 mm thick. Use the string to check that the marzipan is large enough to cover the cake comfortably. Cut off any excess.

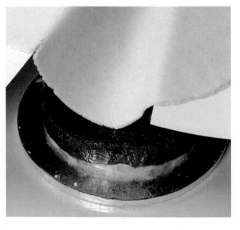

5. Slip the lifters underneath the marzipan, lift it gently and drape it over the cake. Slide out the lifters so that the marzipan falls over the cake.

6. Using a rolling pin, gently roll over the marzipan on the top of the cake and then press the marzipan against the sides of the cake with your hands.

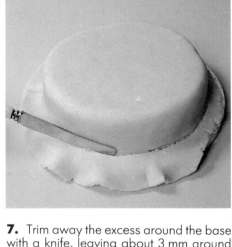

7. Trim away the excess around the base with a knife, leaving about 3 mm around the cake. Still using your knife, press the edges of the marzipan against the base of the cake. Rub the marzipan with both hands to smooth it, taking care not to press too hard as this will leave fingermarks. Hold a set of smoothers firmly against the sides of the cake and rub gently to further smooth the marzipan. Set the cake aside for three or four days so that the marzipan can dry out.

8. Knead and work the plastic icing (page 14) on your pastry board, or a clean, smooth surface in the kitchen, until it is pliable. You may, if you wish, add

25 mℓ liquid glucose to each kilogram of plastic icing to keep it soft for longer. Place the plastic icing in a plastic bag so that it does not dry out.

9. Measure the cake with a length of string, as you did for the marzipan, and tie a knot to mark the correct measurement.

10. Place the cake in a comfortable position and dampen the marzipan (either by wetting your hands and rubbing them over the marzipan, or by using a pastry-brush dipped in water), until it is evenly covered and slightly sticky – but not wet and syrupy. Wipe off any water on the board.

11. Sprinkle the working surface with dry icing sugar. Place the plastic icing onto the icing sugar and roll it out, lifting it occasionally and keeping it to the shape of the cake. Do not turn the icing over. When the icing is of an even thickness, use the string to check that you have the correct size and cut away any excess. Give the icing a good 'polish' with your hands and prick any air bubbles that have emerged.

12. Slide your hands or the lifters under the plastic icing and lift it onto the cake, checking to see that the icing covers the entire surface of the cake.

13. Now, using your hands, gently ease the plastic icing around the cake (if it is a square cake, start with the corners first) without making folds in the icing or tearing it. While you are working, gently rub your hands all over the cake to give a smooth, satiny finish. Trim away any excess icing at the base of the cake.

14. Use a smooth knife and firmly press the icing against the base to give a smooth, even finish.

15. Check all around the cake and smooth over any uneven patches. Use smoothers to further even the sides of the cake.

TO COVER A PLAIN CAKE
To cover a plain cake with plastic icing, spread the cake with smooth apricot jam but omit the marzipan.

TO COVER A SQUARE CAKE

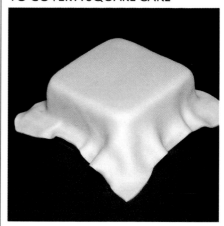

1. Lay the plastic icing over the cake, making sure it will cover the entire cake comfortably.

2. Once the top is flat, smooth and fit the corners by cupping your hand around each corner before doing the sides.

ASSEMBLING TIERS USING PLASTIC PILLARS

1. Once the cake has been covered with plastic icing, work out the position of the pillars. Make a template from paper or thin card by drawing around the cake tin. Fold the template into quarters to find the centre.

2. Mark the position of the pillars on the template by measuring the distance diagonally from the centre. Place the template on the cake and mark the positions with a pin. Remove the template.

Size of cake	Distance of pillar from centre
200 mm	65 mm
250 mm	75 mm
300 mm	90 mm

3. Carefully push a skewer into the cake until the point reaches the cake board. Place the pillar next to the skewer and mark the skewer level with the top of the pillar. Carefully remove the skewer and use this as a measure to cut the remaining skewers to the same length. Insert cut skewers, blunt-end first, into the cake. Place the pillars over the skewers.

ASSEMBLING TIERS USING EXTRUDED ACRYLIC STANDS

1. Place a square or circle of paper over the stand and mark the centre of the pillars on the paper.

2. Place the paper in the centre of the covered cake and mark the positions of the pillars on the cake with a pin. Remove the paper.

3. Insert the pointed end of a skewer into the cake at each of the marked spots until the skewer touches the cake board. Remove the skewer, then re-insert it, blunt-end first, into one of the holes. With a pencil, mark the skewer level with the top of the cake, then remove the skewer and cut it at the marked spot. Cut more skewers to the same length.

4. Place a cut skewer into each of the holes in the cake. The skewers should be about 1 mm below the surface of the cake. Conceal the ends of the skewers with a little royal or plastic icing. Place the extruded acrylic stand on the cake so that the pillars are positioned above each skewer.

The Colour Wheel

Although the subject of colour is vast enough to fill a book in its own right, it is only necessary for the cake decorator to learn the basic principles and from there on experience will teach one the rest. As considerable differences in colour can be noted between mixes of different media, experimentation is essential. For example, brown is usually created by mixing together orange and blue. With food colouring, however, a brown is created by using green and red. Since black and white cannot be created, it is advised that cake decorators use the ready-mixed varieties.

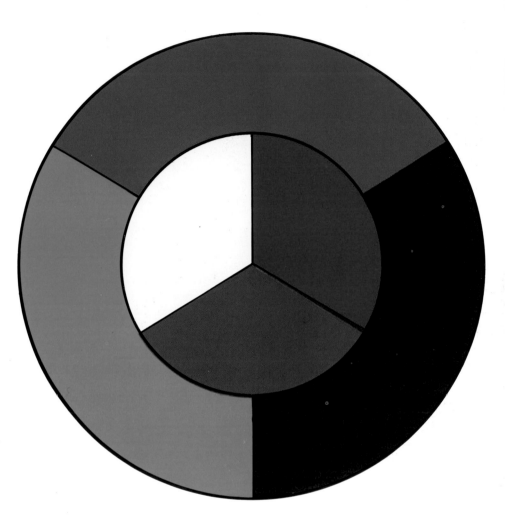

Primary colours are the three basic colours from which all other colours are made. These are red, blue and yellow. Primary colours cannot be created by mixing any other colours together.

Secondary colours are obtained by mixing equal parts of any two primary colours. For example, red and blue make purple, red and yellow make orange, and yellow and blue make green.

Tertiary colours are obtained when secondary and primary colours are mixed together. All shades of all colours, excluding primaries and secondaries, are classed as tertiary colours.

Complementary colours are the two colours that lie opposite each other on the colour wheel. Any two primary colours mixed together will create the complementary colour of the remaining primary colour. Therefore, red and blue make purple, the complementary colour of yellow. Yellow and red make orange, the complementary colour of blue, and yellow and blue make green, which is the complementary colour of red.

Shading is done by using a complementary colour and not by using black. A yellow ball shaded with purple (its complementary colour) will create a three-dimensional effect.

HINTS ON MIXING COLOURS
If you cannot buy the exact shade you require, try mixing your own colours:

Golden-yellow: lemon yellow plus a touch of orange or red.
Lime-green: green plus some yellow.
Sea-green: green plus royal blue.
Brick-red: brown plus red.
Orange: lemon yellow plus red.
Grey: black plus white.
Tan: brown plus white plus a little yellow.
Flesh: pink plus a little yellow.

To lighten any colour, add white.

Paper Cones

*If you are piping in many colours or using different tubes,
make several paper cones before you start working.*

METHOD 1

1. Use a sheet of greaseproof paper measuring approximately 680 x 420 mm. Fold the sheet into three as shown in the diagram and with a smooth-bladed knife slit along the folds.

2. Fold each of these three pieces diagonally into two. Again slit along the fold with a knife. The sheet makes six paper cones.

3. Mark each corner of each triangular sheet as shown with A1, A2 and A3 on one side, and B1, B2 and B3 on the reverse side.

4. Hold points B2 and B1 in your left and right hands respectively. Cross corner B1 onto A2 so that A1 and A3 are facing you. Do not expect the points to be even – they should be crossing each other.

5. Holding crossed points A1 and A2 in your left hand, grasp point A3 in your right hand. Pull point A3 twice around the cone in an anti-clockwise motion.

6. Now pull point B3 sharply upwards to meet points A1 and A2 and grasp all three in your left hand.

7. With your right hand, gently pull points A2 and A3 alternately until you have a very sharp point at the tip of the cone.

8. Fold the tip of point A3 over – in towards the centre of the cone. Fold over again several times – these folds should be small folds approximately 5 mm in width – until all the layers are held firmly. Smooth and press folds until the cone holds its shape firmly. All layers should be flat against one another; there should be no gaps between the layers.

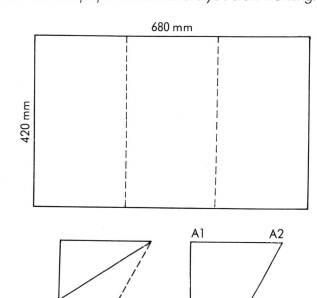

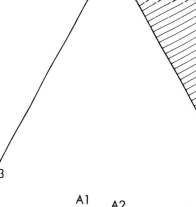

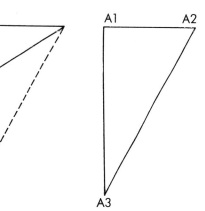

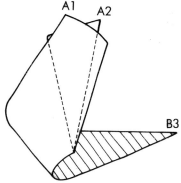

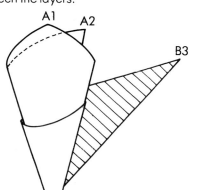

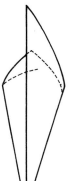

METHOD 2

1. Cut any size square diagonally across to make two triangles.

2. Mark the corners and one side as shown. With the long side of the triangle away from you, roll point C to meet point B and then do the same with point A.

3. Fold points A, B and C inwards, folding them several times to hold the layers firmly.

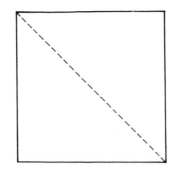

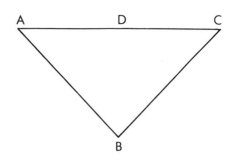

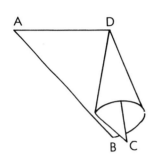
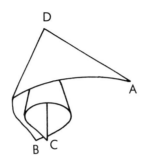

HOW TO FILL THE PAPER CONE

Cut off the tip of the cone approximately 15 mm from the point. Drop an icing tube into the cone – about half the tube should be visible. Let the cone rest in the circle made by thumb and forefinger and place a small amount of icing into the cone with a knife. Try to avoid getting any icing on the edges of the cone. Press the sides of the cone together and fold over the top edge. Then fold the corners towards the centre. Again fold the edges of the cone over a few times. A cone can be refilled and used a few times.

HOW TO HOLD AN ICING CONE

The best way to hold an icing cone (or bag) is in such a way that you can press with your thumb while holding the cone, almost as you would hold a pen or pencil. Learn to press with one hand only, although you may guide with the other.

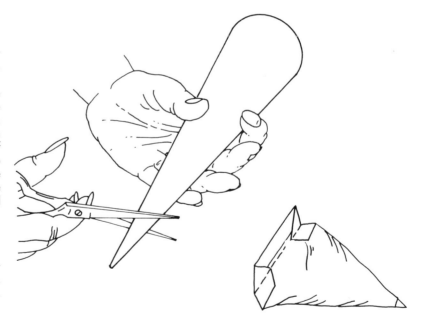

NOTE: When you are not using the filled cone, place the end of the tube into a damp cloth or sponge to prevent the icing hardening and blocking the tube. Do not, however, put the *paper cone* into the wet cloth.

Decorating Techniques

Tubework or piping is an essential part of cake decorating. With practice, you will soon master the fine art of decorating a cake using royal icing and a tube. The following pages will take you step by step through the various basic techniques such as lines, loops, shells, scrolls, embroidery, lace pieces, basket weave and so on. In addition, full colour, step-by-step photographs illustrate simply and clearly the techniques of piping flowers as these are an integral part of this decorative art form.

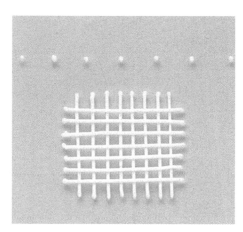
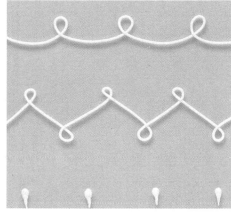

EXERCISES ON GLASS

It is very useful to practise on a sheet of glass as it is easy to keep clean and enables you to make certain of mastering a step or technique before working on an actual cake. Later on, when you begin to learn more difficult designs, a pattern can be placed under the glass which you can follow while working on top.

ICING TUBES

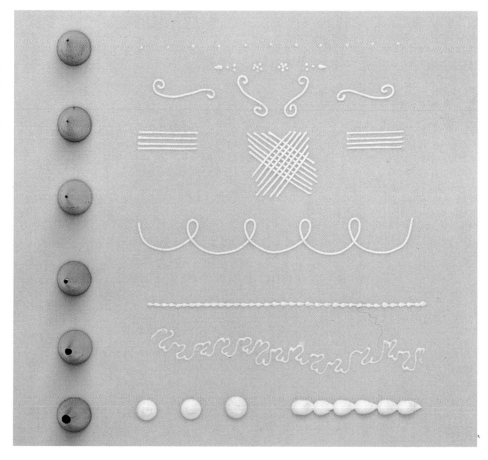

Writing tubes: These are used for writing messages onto cakes, making dots, lines, loops, embroidery (page 24) and also for figure piping (page 35). Generally, these tubes are the lower numbers in the range, for example 00, 0, 1, 2, and so on.

A very useful exercise for piping *lines* and *loops* is to touch the work surface with the end of the tube, press on the cone and then lift the tube about 40 to 45 mm away from the glass or cake, pressing constantly and not stretching the icing, so that the icing falls into place on the surface.

When forming *dots and beads*, it is difficult to disguise the tail. For small dots, the icing should be soft. Use very little pressure on the cone, just enough to make a tiny dot. For larger dots use constant pressure and keep the point of the tube stationary in the bead or dot until it is the size required. Release pressure and move the cone gently in a circle before removing the tube. Gently press any projecting point down into the dot or bead, if necessary.

Cornelli or scribbling is done with No. 00, 0 or 1 writing tubes using a maze of Ws and Ms in a continuous line but at random. You should not be able to see where the work begins or ends.

Star tubes: There is a very large range of star tubes available. These are used for making shells, stars, scrolls and so on. Make sure the icing is the correct consistency – it should form a firm peak when a knife is lifted out of the icing.

To create *stars* hold the cone, fitted with the appropriate tube, perpendicular to the surface. Press the cone firmly to release the icing, stop pressing, then remove the cone.

To form *shells*, use any of the star tubes available and hold the icing cone at a 45° angle. With the tip of the tube touching the surface of the work, press very firmly. Move the tube slightly away from the surface giving the icing room to build up. Ease off pressing, then stop pressing, tapering off the icing by pulling the cone towards you. You have now formed the first shell. Now, just touching on the end of the first, start the next shell, ensuring that the untidy start of the icing does not show and again, pressing very firmly, repeat the procedure.

To create *pull-up shells* around the side of a cake, repeat the same procedure in an upwards direction.

Rosettes are piped with a deep-cut star tube, that is either a Probus No. 13 or Ateco No. 33, moved in a circular motion,

Petal tubes: These can be either straight, such as Probus No. 42 or Ateco No. 101, or curved, such as the Bekenal No. 57, and are used for any royal icing flowers such as roses, daisies, and so on. An exception is the horseshoe shape, Ateco No. 81, used for chrysanthemums and lily-of-the-valley. (See pages 32-34 on how to pipe different flowers.)

Drop flower tubes, which make a whole flower with one pressing of the icing cone, are also available in many varieties, for example Probus No. 31 and Ateco No. 224. My favourite is the Bekenal No. 37 drop flower tube as it is very easy to use and is most effective on children's cakes (see page 33 for details).

Special effect tubes: For a shell and ruffle border, the Ateco Nos. 86, 87 and 88 are very effective. The grass or hair tube, Ateco No. 233, is very useful on children's cakes. Multiple hole tubes can be used most successfully in various ways, for example there is one with five holes in a row which can be used for writing music lines on a cake.

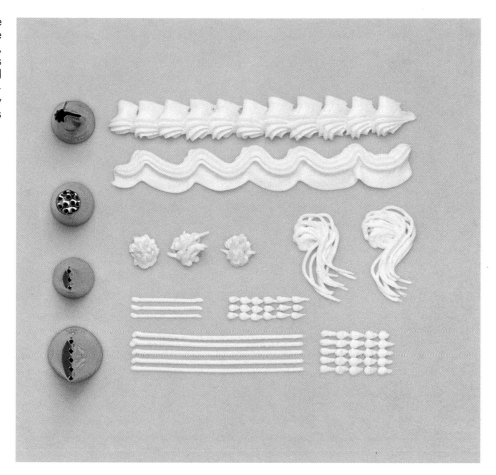

Ribbon tubes: One or both edges are serrated and these can be used for piping ribbons or bands and also for basket weave, for example Bekenal No. 22. Included here is the curved tube, Ateco No. 98 (sometimes referred to as a shell tube) which is the one I like to use for basket weave (page 28).

Leaf tubes: While one can use a paper cone to pipe leaves, there are very good leaf tubes available in three sizes, namely the Ateco Nos. 349, 350 and 352.

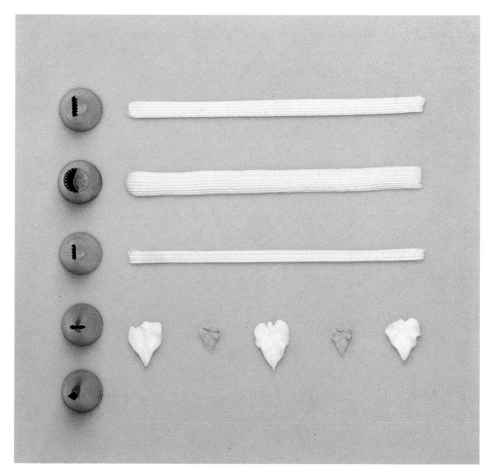

EMBROIDERY

The fine designs piped onto the side of a cake are commonly called 'embroidery'. This is best done with one of the fine writing tubes and royal icing with a 'soft peak' consistency.

The design can be done free-hand on the cake or, if you wish, pricked out using a tracing. This latter method has its disadvantages, however, as the pinpricks will show. The method I use is to prick only the centres of the little flowers and then add the stems and leaves. Another method is to use a glass stencil (page 28) to transfer the design onto fresh icing.

It is advisable to make a very simple embroidery design on the cake initially and later, when you feel more confident, to try a more complicated design. Patterns for embroidery designs can be found on page 160.

1. Fill a small writing tube with royal icing and pipe the embroidery design by first piping the centre dot of each flower.

2. Then pipe the five dots around each centre, and lastly, the stems and leaves.

PICOT EDGE

1. Fill a No. 0 or 1 writing tube with royal icing and pipe a row of small dots.

2. Pipe three dots opposite the spaces next to the first four dots.

3. Pipe two dots opposite the spaces next to the three dots and then one dot between the two dots.

4. Miss one dot in the original row of dots and repeat Steps 2 and 3 to create the picot effect.

BRUSH EMBROIDERY

This interesting and effective technique uses royal icing to which a little water has been added or, alternatively, 2 mℓ piping jelly, liquid glucose or glycerine may be added to one mixture of royal icing.

The glass stencil method is ideal for transferring the design onto the cake but, to avoid a mirror image of your design, trace onto the back of the pattern and then follow that with royal icing in a No. 0 writing tube.

1. Fill a No. 1 or 2 writing tube with the royal icing and with extra pressure, pipe a line around a petal or leaf.

2. Hold a 2 mm wide flat brush at an angle of approximately 45 ° and brush the icing from the outer edge inwards. Follow the veins of the petals or leaves. Leave the outer edge thicker, fading away to the centre or lower point.

3. Work on a small section at a time to prevent the icing from drying before you have brushed it. Small details, such as dots for stamens, may be piped in afterwards once the brush embroidery has set.

LACE PIECES

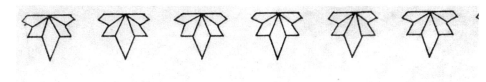

Because they are so fragile and break easily, lace pieces are usually the last decoration to be added to a cake. Patterns of various lace pieces can be found on page 161.

1. Copy the design onto a piece of tracing paper using a sharp pencil or fine felt-tip pen.

2. Tape the four corners of the tracing paper to a work surface and tape a larger piece of waxed paper over the pattern. Use only a couple of pieces of tape so that you do not disturb the lace pieces too much when you remove the tape.

3. Pipe the lace pieces onto the waxed paper using a small writing tube. Wipe the end of the tube with a damp cloth while piping each piece to ensure clean lines. Always make more pieces than are needed to allow for breakages. Allow the pieces to dry for at least two hours.

4. Remove the lace by placing the waxed paper over the index finger of your left hand. The lace will start to lift. Gently lift it off between thumb and forefinger. Do not attempt to lift the lace pieces off with tweezers as the slightest pressure will break the lace.

5. Use a small writing tube to make a 20 mm row of dots on the cake. Press the straight edge of the lace piece into the centre of the dots to secure it. Continue to attach the other lace pieces in the same way, then gently push each piece so that it slopes slightly downwards.

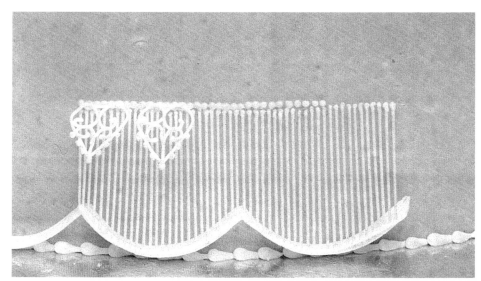

EXTENSION WORK

This is a method of bordering a cake. The depth of regular or basic extension work should be about one third of the height of the cake or about 33 mm deep. It is advisable not to make the extension work too deep to start with as the longer the lines, the more difficult they are to do.

1. Cut a strip of greaseproof paper as wide as the depth of your cake and as long as its circumference. Draw two pencil lines along the length of the paper 33 mm and 10 mm from one edge.

2. Fold the paper in half by putting the two ends together, then fold again and continue in this way until the paper is folded into a piece about 30 mm wide. Open out the paper strip and put it around the cake with the 10 mm line close to the cake board and then stick the ends together with sticky tape. On a square cake, see that there is a fold of the paper on each corner. Now make a pinprick at 33 mm and 10 mm on each fold line round the cake.

3. Remove the greaseproof paper and rule a line on the cake with a pin, joining together the upper pinpricks. At this point embroidery is done on the sides of the cake.

4. Fill a writing tube (any size from 00 to 3) with royal icing (the icing should be the same consistency used for making shells) and make a continuous row of beading around the base of the cake where it meets the board. Allow to set.

5. Fill a writing tube (any size from 00 to 3) with royal icing and pipe the first 'support row' by touching the tube to the first of the 10 mm pinpricks. Move to the next 10 mm pinprick, pressing the cone and letting the icing fall into a scallop between the marks. Taper off each scallop at the beginning and end so that the icing is not too thick. Continue in this way right around the cake.

It is absolutely essential that you do not let the icing scallops touch the board. Any movement in the board could crack the extension work and a whole section could be damaged. Allow this first row of scallops to dry partially for about half an hour.

6. Do another support row of scallops by piping directly onto the first row. When you look at the scallops at eye level, they should appear as a single line.

7. When the second row of scallops is complete, allow it to firm before adding the third row of scallops. Additional rows of scallops may be added, if desired. (Adding a new row while the previous one is still wet may make the whole lot collapse.) Leave for approximately 24 hours to allow these support rows to dry thoroughly before continuing the extension work.

8. Using a small writing tube, pipe a line from the 33 mm line to a point where two scallops meet. Then pipe a line to the deepest point of the scallop and a third line to the point where this scallop joins the next one. Then, pressing firmly, pipe a series of lines from the 33 mm line to the edge of the scallop – make sure that each line remains taut. The space between the drop lines should be the width of a line – you should not be able to fit more than one line between the drop lines. Continue in this way right around the cake.

9. With the same tube, pipe a line over the end of the drop lines on the scallop to neaten off the base of the extension work.

NOTE: If the icing keeps breaking, the reason may be either that you are not pressing firmly and consistently on the cone, or that the icing is too soft – it is very important to have your icing the correct consistency. Finally, the icing may be too stiff, in which case add a few drops of water or egg white or, preferably, mix a fresh batch.

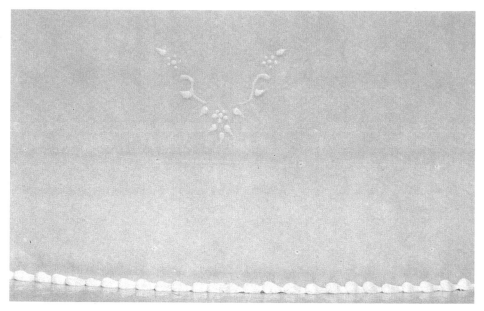

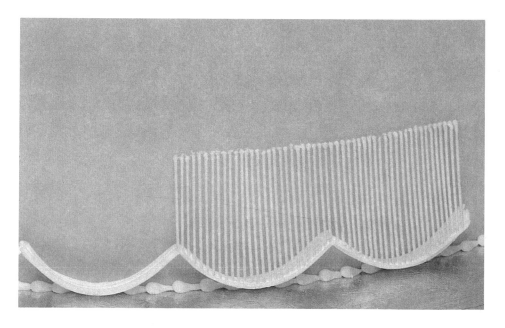

GLASS STENCILS

I have found this technique invaluable for transferring embroidery designs, lettering or pictures onto a cake.

1. Trace the design onto a piece of paper. Carefully outline the design on the back of the paper with a pencil.

2. Place the design under the glass so that the pencilled outlines are facing you. Fill a paper cone with royal icing and, using a small writing tube, pipe directly onto the glass (the lettering or design will be back-to-front). Allow the icing to dry.

3. When the icing is quite hard, press the design against fresh plastic icing. Lift the glass away and you will have the design on your cake exactly where you want it.

BASKET WEAVE

Weaving is achieved by using a ribbon tube (where one edge is serrated and the other straight) and royal icing.

1. Pipe a vertical line the required length onto the work surface, then do a number of short lines across the first vertical line, leaving a space the width of your tube between them.

2. Now do another vertical line, just covering the ends of the short ones.

3. Pipe short lines over this vertical line so that the start of your short line looks as though it is coming from underneath the first long vertical line. Continue in this way, filling in all the spaces along the last vertical line. Repeat this procedure until you have covered the area required.

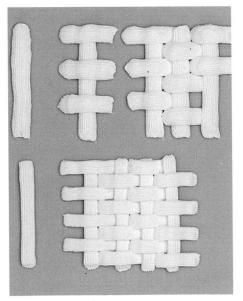

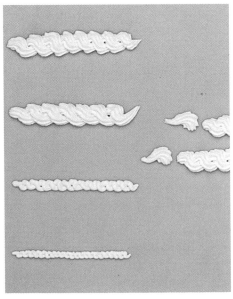

ROPING

1. Fill a cone with royal icing and use a small or medium star tube, or a large writing tube, to create a twisted rope. Hold the cone at a 45° angle and pipe a 'comma' curving downwards, then to the left, flicking slightly to the right as you end off. Keep constant pressure on the cone as you work.

FLOODWORK

Floodwork, or run-in-work, is the art of filling in a picture with royal icing thinned to the right consistency. It is advisable to do more than one picture at a time so that, while one section is drying, you can work on a section in another picture. Floodwork items will keep very well in a strong box protected from dust and bumps.

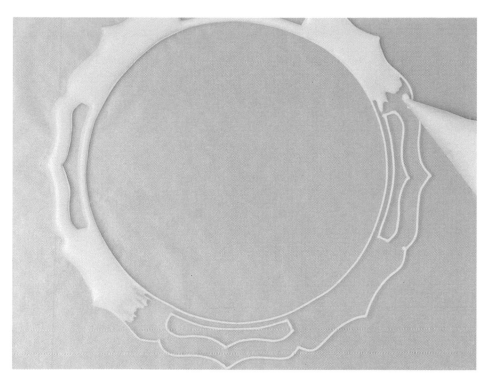

Mix royal icing to a firm peak consistency and then thin down half of it with a few drops of water. Use an eye dropper to get the consistency exactly right. Do not beat the icing when adding the water but stir it gently. It is preferable to allow the icing to stand for 12 hours so that any bubbles can subside.

When a knife is drawn through it, the thinned icing should only come together after a slow count of ten. Icing which is too thin does not set well.

It is important to dry floodwork quickly to retain its shine. If you are working on a rainy day, use a heater or the warming drawer to dry the floodwork.

1. Place the picture to be flooded under glass and stick it in place at the corners with a little royal icing. Tape a piece of waxed (not greaseproof) paper to the glass, ensuring that there is at least a 20 mm margin around the edge of the picture. Do make sure that there are no wrinkles in the paper. If the design has a middle opening (like a collar, for example) you may cut a small cross in the centre of the paper to relax the natural tension of the paper. Any buckling or wrinkling of the paper may cause the design to break.

2. Outline the picture using firm peak royal icing in a small writing tube.

3. Fill a paper cone with thinned icing, but do not cut the hole in the bottom until you are ready to fill in the design otherwise the icing will flow out. It is not necessary to use a tube. Make sure the hole is not too big, or the icing may flow out too quickly, overrunning your lines. Start close to your outline, but do not touch it with the cone as it may break. Always start filling in the part of the picture that is furthest away from you. For example, of two trees one behind the other, you would do the back one first.

Keep the tip of the bag close to the surface to reduce the formation of air bubbles and let the icing flow out, moving the bag backwards and forwards across the shape.

4. When flooding a collar for a cake, flood a section and then flood alternately on either side of that section. This prevents the icing from setting and leaving a line.

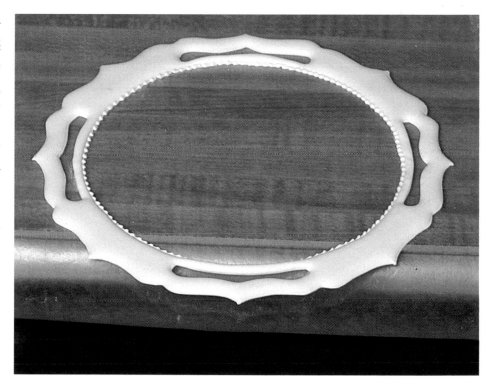

5. When the area is almost filled, use a small paintbrush to push the icing to the outline to form a smooth edge. If any bubbles appear, immediately smooth them away with a paintbrush or hatpin.

6. Once the floodwork is dry, slide the piece of paper with the floodwork onto the edge of the table. Gently pull the paper downwards against the edge of the table while supporting the floodwork with your other hand. Keep turning the picture so that the paper is removed evenly all round. Do not extend the floodwork more than 50% beyond the table edge.

7. To attach a collar, pipe a line of icing with a No. 2 writing tube all around the top edge of the cake and then position the collar on this line. When positioning smaller pieces on a cake, it is easier to paint the back of the floodwork piece with royal icing before attaching it.

PIPED FLOWERS

Unfortunately, since the popularity of moulded flowers, piped flowers have lost much of their glamour. This is a great shame as they are fun to make, involve a certain amount of skill and, apart from that, can be attractively used in a variety of ways on Easter eggs, children's birthday cakes and novelties and to decorate pastillage cards, ornaments and plaques.

APPLE BLOSSOM FLOWER, BUD AND LEAF

EQUIPMENT
medium petal tube
white, pink and green royal icing
   (page 14)
small writing tube or plain cone
40 mm square waxed paper
flower nail

1. Fill a medium petal tube with pink and white icing, placing the pink icing on the side of the cone to line up with the wider opening of the petal tube and then adding the white icing. Fill a small writing tube, or a plain cone cut to size, with green icing. Fix a small square of waxed paper to the top of the flower nail with a touch of icing.

BLOSSOM
1. Hold the flower nail in your left hand (right if left-handed). In the other hand, hold the tube of pink and white icing at an angle of about 30° to the surface of the nail with the wider opening, where the pink icing is, to the centre of the nail. The narrow opening in the tube must be slightly raised from the nail.

2. Press the cone, moving the tube very slightly towards the outer edge of the nail and at the same time, turning the nail very slightly in an anti-clockwise direction (clockwise for left-handers). Now move the tube back towards the centre of the nail and stop turning and pressing. This is the first petal of the apple blossom which has five petals.

3. Repeat four more petals, starting each new petal slightly under the preceding one. Take care with the last petal and lift the cone, not the tube, slightly higher, to about a 45° angle, so as not to damage the previous petals.

4. Use the cone containing the green icing and pipe five very small dots close to each other in the centre of the complete flower.

5. Remove the waxed paper very carefully from the flower nail. Hold a corner between thumb and forefinger and then slide the middle finger underneath the paper to support the flower. Place it in a box or on a piece of glass to dry.

BUD (or slightly-opened flower)
1. Pipe three petals as you did for the blossom flower.

2. Turn the flower nail so that the three petals are facing you upside down. With a small writing tube filled with green icing, pipe a teardrop starting from the base of the first petal and finishing close to the top of the petal. Repeat on the other two petals to form the calyx.

3. Turn the nail so that the petals are the right way up. Place the tube into the base of the calyx and press very firmly to form a bulb, then taper away into a stem.

> **NOTE:** To make a smaller bud, make only two petals and do exactly the same as described above. These buds help to 'soften' the arrangement of flowers on a cake.

LEAF
1. Fill a plain cone with green royal icing and cut the cone to form a leaf shape. A leaf tube can also be used.

2. Press firmly and allow the icing to build up. Reduce pressure and pull the tube away, tapering the end of the leaf.

> **NOTE:** These leaves can be made in advance and allowed to dry or they can be piped directly onto a cake and used to attach the royal icing flowers.

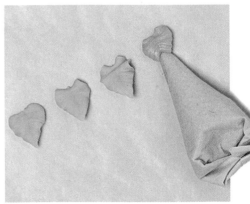

DAISY

EQUIPMENT
white and yellow royal icing (page 14)
medium petal tube
small writing tube
40 mm square waxed paper
flower nail

Two types of daisy can be piped.

1. Colour a quarter of the icing yellow. Fill a cone with a medium petal tube and white royal icing and another with a small writing tube and yellow icing. Attach a square of waxed paper to the flower nail with a dot of royal icing.

METHOD 1
1. With the medium petal tube and white icing, pipe a series of petals as you did for the apple blossom, but make each petal slightly longer. Do not forget that the wider opening in the tube must be facing towards the centre of the nail. The daisy can have any number of petals.

2. Make a large dot in the centre of the flower using the small writing tube and yellow icing. Remove the flower and the waxed paper square from the nail and set it aside to dry.

METHOD 2
1. Hold the tube containing white icing just above the surface of the nail and at right angles to it, with the wider opening in the tube towards the centre of the nail.

Start about 10 mm from the centre of the nail and press firmly, moving the tube to the centre of the nail. Continue in this way, working in a circle. Any number of petals may be used for this flower, but they must be of even thickness and close together. Take care not to 'stretch' the icing as this results in thin petals which break very easily when removed from the waxed paper.

Do not turn the flower nail when piping a petal of this flower.

2. When the petals are complete, pipe a yellow dot in the centre of the flower using the writing tube. Remove the flower and the waxed paper from the nail and set it aside to dry.

DROP FLOWERS

Drop flowers, most suitable for use on children's cakes, are piped in one action using a special tube. A Bekenal No. 37 tube is my favourite.

1. Hold the cone of icing, with the tube in it, at right angles close to the work surface. Press so that enough icing shows to form an attractive flower. Stop pressing before lifting the tube away from the icing.

2. Pipe centres with yellow icing in a small writing tube and pipe the leaves with a paper cone cut to shape or use a leaf tube.

> **NOTE:** Some drop flowers require a twist of the wrist as one is pressing the cone.

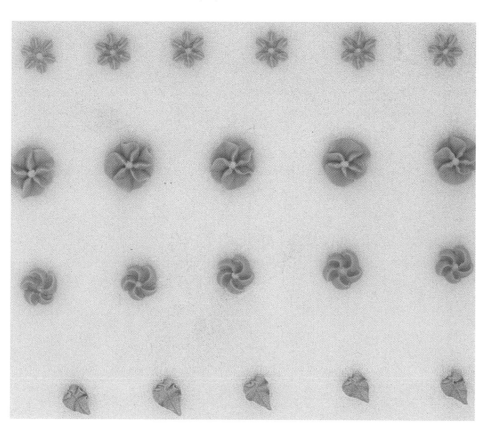

ROSE FLOWER AND BUD

EQUIPMENT
40 mm square waxed paper
flower nail
large petal tube
250 mℓ pale pink royal icing (page 14)

1. Attach the waxed paper to the flower nail with a dot of royal icing. Fill a large petal tube and a paper cone with pale pink icing.

2. Hold the tube against the waxed paper on the flower nail and at right angles to it. With the wide end of the tube to the centre of the nail, press the cone, and when the icing comes through, pull the cone towards you as though you are pulling down a lever. When the side of the tube is touching the nail, turn the nail in your left hand (right hand if left-handed) in a clockwise direction (anti-clockwise if left handed) allowing the icing to wrap around the icing already on the nail, thus forming a cone.

3. End off by turning the nail but holding the tube steady in the one position until you have completely circled the cone.

Stop pressing and turn the nail and pull the tube away in the same direction ending low on the cone and close to the nail.

4. Continue building this cone of icing by wrapping another 'band' of icing around the icing on the nail. Hold the paper cone at a 45° angle with the tube close to the top of the icing on the nail and almost touching it. This cone will form the centre of the rose. Repeat this process once more so that the cone is 15 mm high.

5. Touch the wide end of the tube to the flower cone about halfway up, with the narrow part of the tube towards your left and away from the icing. Press and turn your right hand from the wrist to the right in an 'up and over' movement, rather like opening a fan. Pipe two more in this way.

6. Hold the tube in the same position as for the first three petals, but start at the base of the cone, in line with the centre of the first petal, right against the nail. Move up and over, turning your hand from the wrist from left to right and finish the petal in line with the centre of the next petal of the previous row. Pipe two more petals in the same way.

7. You have now completed the rose. Carefully remove the waxed paper and rose from the nail and set it aside to dry thoroughly.

ROSEBUD
1. Proceed as for the rose flower, but after the first three petals shake the nail gently so that the cone falls onto its side and the 'V' formed by two of the petals is facing you.

2. Use a hatpin to cut away the excess icing on either side of the base of the bud.

> **NOTE:** The rose can be piped directly onto a toothpick instead of onto a flower nail. Touch the end of the toothpick in some white margarine or vegetable fat and then pipe the rose directly onto it. Remove gently when the flower has set.

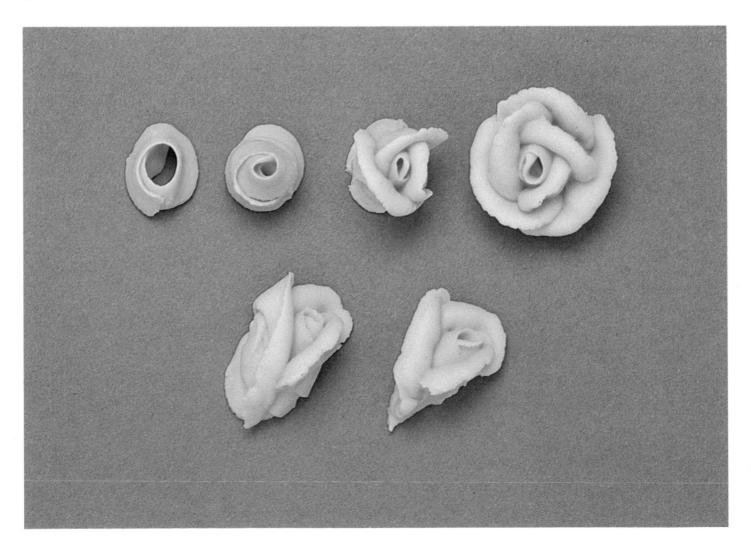

FIGURE PIPING

Figure piping may be executed with any size writing tube but, of course, the size of the tube will determine the size of the figure. Use royal icing that is firm enough to hold its shape when piped into a ball but not so stiff as to form ridges. No patterns are required as figure piping is done freehand. Use constant pressure and keep the end of the tube in the icing while piping.

Tiny teddy bear: Use a No. 0 writing tube and royal icing and pipe the body, head, arms, legs and ears, in that order, onto a piece of waxed paper. When the teddy is dry, remove it and attach it to the cake with royal icing.

Bunny: Using white royal icing in a No. 2 writing tube, pipe the bunny as shown onto waxed paper and allow it to dry. Remove the bunny and attach it to the cake with royal icing.

Baby face: Pipe the face onto waxed paper with soft flesh-coloured royal icing in a No. 3 or 4 writing tube and allow it to dry thoroughly. Paint the eyes and mouth with food colouring. With white royal icing in a No. 3 or 4 writing tube, pipe a large ball onto waxed paper to form the bonnet. Immediately attach the face by pushing it into this ball. If desired, trim the bonnet with tiny royal icing dots using a No. 0 or 1 writing tube and leave it to dry thoroughly.

RIBBON BOWS

Ribbon bows made from florist ribbon are very useful decorations for celebration cakes. They are usually made from strips of ribbon about half a metre long and of any width. Make a few bows in different sizes and colours and keep them ready for use.

1. Cut a length of ribbon 500 mm long and 10 mm wide. At one end make a loop about 30 mm long so that the end hangs below the short one.

2. Fold the long end so that the right side is uppermost, then make another loop to form the other half of the bow.

3. Fold underneath again so that the right side is uppermost and continue until no more loops can be made.

4. Cut a length of wire about 50 mm long and bend it over the centre of the ribbon to hold the latter firmly together, then twist the wire tightly.

5. Pull the loops so that they all point in the same direction.

6. Curl the loose end of the bow using the blade of a pair of scissors. Attach the bow to the cake with royal icing, by inserting it into a small mound of plastic icing or by taping it to flower sprays.

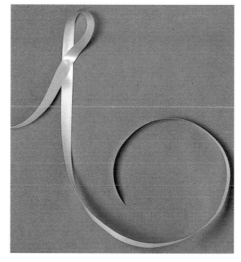

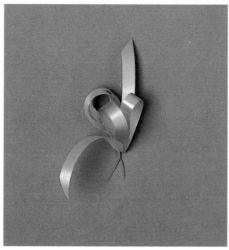

RIBBON INSERTION

Ribbon insertion is used very effectively with embroidery and as an attractive side decoration on cakes.

It is important to cut the ribbon slots while the plastic icing is still fresh.

1. Cut a piece of greaseproof paper the same height as the cake and long enough to go right around the cake. Join the ends together with tape and slip it off the cake.

2. Flatten the paper and press in the folds so that the paper is double.

3. Fold the paper in half lengthwise, then open it up and draw a pencil line along this fold.

4. Now draw two more lines, one about 5 mm above the centre line and one 5 mm below.

5. Measure the length of the paper and mark even spaces with pencil dots along the centre pencil line.

6. Replace the paper around the cake and, with a pin, carefully make two pin-pricks on the top and bottom lines in line with the pencil dots.

7. Remove the paper and cut vertical slots into the plastic icing with a ribbon inserter (or hobby knife) to join the pin-pricks.

There are several methods of inserting ribbons. Here are four examples.

EXAMPLE A
1. Use 10 mm wide ribbon and cut it into 25 mm long pieces.

2. With the ribbon inserter, cut slots into the plastic icing at approximately 20 mm intervals.

3. Slot a piece of ribbon into every alternate space.

EXAMPLE B
1. Use 10 mm wide very soft, satin ribbon and cut it into 15 mm long pieces.

2. Cut slots at 25 mm intervals with a ribbon inserter. Bend the ribbon in half and insert both ends into the same slot.

EXAMPLE C
1. Cut 10 mm wide ribbon into 50 mm lengths and cut a 'V' out of each end.

2. Cut pairs of slots into the icing anything from 5 to 10 mm apart with a space of 25 mm between them.

3. Insert the ribbon into the two slots, leaving approximately 20 mm of the ends showing.

EXAMPLE D
1. Cut 10 mm wide ribbon into 35 mm lengths and cut a 'V' out of one end. Cut the other end at an angle. Cut 12 mm lengths of the same ribbon.

2. Cut pairs of slots into the icing 10 mm apart at 25 mm intervals. Insert the pieces of ribbon into the prepared slots.

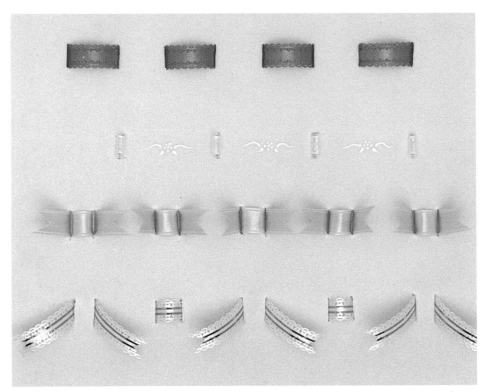

SUGAR MOULDING

This is one of the simplest of cake decorating techniques that produces delightful results.

INGREDIENTS
500 mℓ castor sugar
20 mℓ water

1. Mix the castor sugar and water together thoroughly with a fork to ensure that there are no lumps.

2. Spoon the mixture into the mould, press down well, then turn out. Tap gently on the top if necessary, to release it.

> **NOTE:** To colour the sugar, add a few drops of food colouring to the water before mixing it with the sugar.

CRIMPING

This is a method of creating patterns by pinching plastic icing together with the use of a crimper. Crimpers come in several designs, but two of the most pleasing and easy to use are the V-shape and the single scallop.

When doing crimping work, especially on a square cake, measure the edge along which you are going to crimp and divide it by the width of the crimper to check that the row will fit perfectly. Always work on freshly applied plastic icing. The crimper ends must be held close together to avoid long 'drag' lines when you pinch the icing. Crimping should always be finished off with royal icing.

1. Dip the ends of the crimper into cornflour. Hold the crimper between thumb and forefinger, with your middle finger as a guide. The ends should be some 5 mm apart.

2. Insert the crimper into the icing. Press the ends together until there is about 2 mm between them. Open the crimpers slightly and remove them.

3. Keep dipping the ends of the crimper in cornflour to prevent them sticking to the icing. Continue in this way along the section you wish to crimp. Decorate with royal icing.

> **NOTE:** If you have difficulty in holding the ends of the crimper close together, put a strong elastic band around the crimper to keep the ends about 5 mm apart.

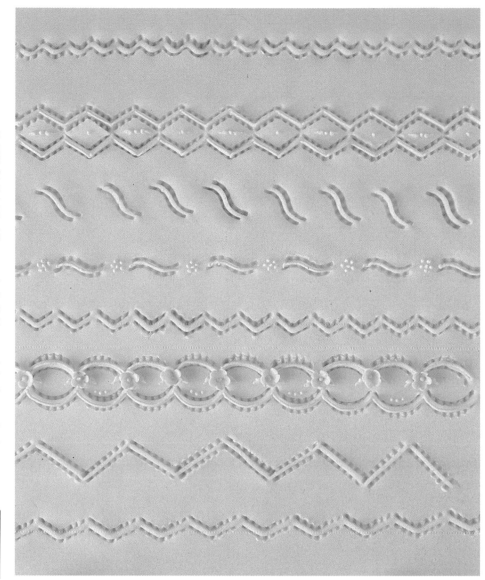

1. Fill a bell mould, or metal or plastic Christmas bell with the clapper removed, with the sugar mixture. Pack it in firmly. Turn it out immediately and allow it to dry for thirty minutes. The smaller the bell, the quicker the sugar will dry.

2. Gently lift the sugar bell in your left hand and, using a small spoon, hollow out the inside of the bell. If you wish, return the bell to the mould while you hollow it out. Set the bell aside carefully to dry thoroughly.

3. Pipe a little royal icing inside the bell and attach a silver ball for a clapper.

> **NOTE:** Children's sand moulds can be used very successfully in sugar moulding as can other hollow objects around the house.

MOULDED FLOWERS

The moulded flowers shown here are used on the cakes in this book or given as alternatives. Moulding flowers is a technique that produces beautiful and realistic results. The ideal way to achieve perfection, however, is to work from nature.

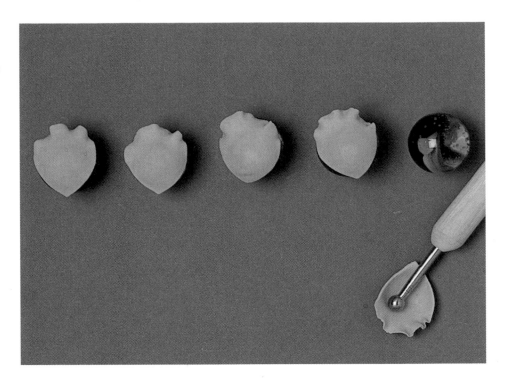

BRIAR ROSE AND LEAF

EQUIPMENT
pale pink, yellow and green modelling paste (page 14)
pattern for rose petals and leaves (page 158)
painting knife
medium ball tool
marbles
vegetable fat
stamens
hollow mould
egg white
leaf veiner

1. Roll out the modelling paste thinly and cut out five rose petals.

2. Pick up a petal with a painting knife and place it onto the heel of your hand with the rounded part of the petal away from your palm. Cover the remaining petals with thin plastic.

3. With a medium ball tool, press firmly around the edge of the petal to thin and flute it slightly. Lift the petal and place it in the centre of your palm.

4. Use the ball tool gently to work the centre of the petal to hollow it. Place the petal over a marble to set. Repeat the procedure on the next four petals. Do not let the petals dry completely otherwise assembly will be difficult.

5. Cut 10 mm off each end of a number of stamens. Press a piece of yellow modelling paste the size of half a pea against a piece of tulle or net. Push the stamens into the yellow centre all around the edge and curl the stamens slightly.

6. Put a little vegetable fat in the centre of a hollow mould. Take the first petal, which should still be pliable, and paint egg white on the righthand straight edge of the petal. Place this petal on the fat in the hollow of the mould. Repeat the procedure with the next four petals, overlapping them by about 5 mm and lifting the first petal over the last.

7. Paint a little egg white into the centre of the petals and attach the yellow centre with the stamens.

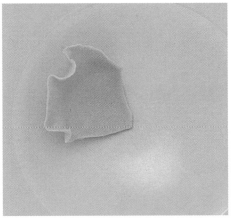

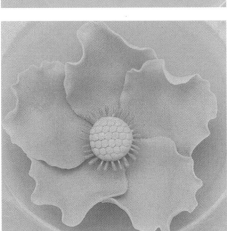

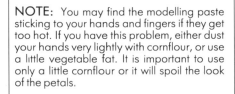

NOTE: You may find the modelling paste sticking to your hands and fingers if they get too hot. If you have this problem, either dust your hands very lightly with cornflour, or use a little vegetable fat. It is important to use only a little cornflour or it will spoil the look of the petals.

LEAF
Roll out green modelling paste thinly and cut out the leaves. Vein the leaves with a plastic or rubber veiner. Pinch the leaves very lightly at their base and place them on a curved shape to dry. Never let leaves dry absolutely flat otherwise they look too stiff in an arrangement.

ROSE AND BUD

EQUIPMENT
florist wire
florist tape
pale pink, pale and dark green modelling paste (page 14)
patterns for calyx and rose petals (page 158)
egg white
ball tool
small scissors

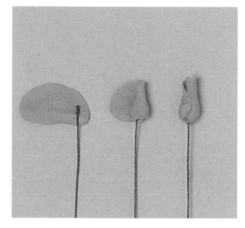

1. Cut green florist tape into four, cover a piece of florist wire and bend over one end. Roll pale pink modelling paste, the size of a large pea, into a ball. Roll into a 'sausage' and then flatten along the length of this roll, flattening one side only.

2. Dip the curved end of the covered florist wire into egg white and place it into one end of the modelling paste. Roll the modelling paste against itself to make a centre for the rose. Set aside to dry.

3. Add the calyx at this stage to form a rosebud. *If a half rose is desired, continue from Step 9 for instructions on how to mould the petals.* Colour modelling paste green and add a touch of brown. Now take a small portion of this paste and add white to it to form a very pale green. Roll out each shade separately, then place one on top of the other, attaching the two layers with egg white if necessary.

4. Roll out the two layers together and cut out the calyx using a calyx cutter or a calyx pattern. Lift the calyx with a painting knife and place it, dark side up, onto the palm of your hand.

5. Move the small end of a ball tool along the length of each sepal and then hollow out the centre of the calyx. Pinch the ends of each sepal to make a point. With small scissors cut a tiny strip away from the base of each sepal.

6. Turn the calyx over and paint egg white on its centre and a little way along each sepal.

7. Join the calyx to the rose by pushing the wire stem through the centre of the calyx. The light side goes against the rose.

8. Roll a piece of darker green paste into a ball the size of a small pea. Flatten one side slightly, paint the flattened side with egg white and push the wire stem through the ball, flat side uppermost, to form the hip of the rose.

9. Roll out pink modelling paste and cut out 3 smaller rose petals with a petal cutter or use a pattern and a sharp knife. Place a petal in the palm of your hand and hollow and flute it with a ball tool.

10. Paint the base of each petal with egg white and attach each to the cone, curving the edges outward. Set aside to dry. Following Steps 3-8 above, add the calyx at this stage to form a half rose.

11. For a fuller rose, cut out five larger petals and hollow and flute the petals with a ball tool in the palm of your hand. Paint with egg white and attach to the cone with the three petals attached. Add the calyx, following Steps 3-8 above, and gently curve back the sepals of the calyx.

HYACINTHS AND FILLER FLOWERS

All bell-shaped flowers are made in the same way, although the number of petals will vary.

EQUIPMENT
modelling paste (page 14)
paintbrush
flower cutter
anger tool
covered florist wire
egg white

1. Use a piece of modelling paste the size of a pea and roll it into a ball. Shape it into a 'hat-shape' with your fingers, then place the wide part on a board and thin the paste using the handle of a paintbrush.

2. Place a flower cutter over the long centre part and cut out the desired shape. Turn the flower over and hollow the inside with an anger tool.

3. Mark each petal with a pin by making a line along its length. Bend over the end of a piece of covered florist wire, dip it into egg white and thread it through the flower. This will enable you to wire small flowers together in sprays. Stamens may be added if desired.

FORGET-ME-NOTS

EQUIPMENT
modelling paste (page 14)
flower cutter
ball tool
stamens or thin covered fuse wire
egg white

1. Roll out the modelling paste and cut out the flowers with a flower cutter.

2. Hollow each flower slightly with a ball tool.

3. Dip the stamen, or thin covered fuse wire, into egg white and insert it into the centre of the flower.

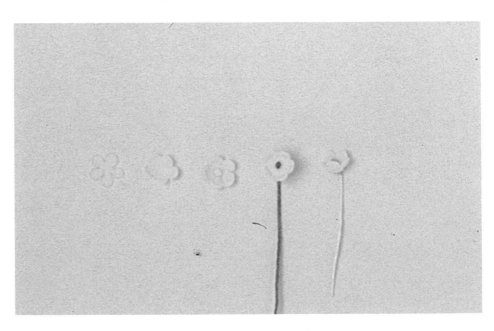

CARNATION

EQUIPMENT
modelling paste (page 14)
icing knife
anger tool
egg white
covered florist wire
green florist tape
paintbrush
food colouring
white stamens

1. To make a small flower, roll out the modelling paste thinly and cut out a scalloped round approximately 50 mm in diameter. Using an icing knife, hobby knife or small scissors, cut tiny 1 mm cuts into the paste all round the edge.

2. Frill the edge of the circle with an anger tool. Paint a cross on the modelling paste with egg white and pinch the centre of the circle from underneath to form a point, making sure that the edges do not stick to one another. Open up the flower with your anger tool to give it a 'fluffy' appearance.

3. Push a piece of 26 g covered florist wire, with a looped end, through the flower and allow it to dry. When dry, you may tape a piece of green florist tape around the base.

4. To make a large flower, repeat Steps 1 and 2 above three or four times and then join the parts together with egg white, pressing them together to form a large carnation. (Touch the edges of the petals with a paintbrush dipped in red or pink food colouring, if desired.)

5. Hollow out a ball of green modelling paste, half the size of a marble, into a cup shape. Thin the edge with your fingers and then cut it into five equal sections. Cut each section into a pointed shape. Thread a piece of covered florist wire, with a closed hook at one end, through the calyx

and then stick a small ball of green paste on top of the wire inside the calyx to secure it. Paint the inside of the calyx with egg white. Attach the calyx to the flower by inserting the completed flower into the hollowed calyx.

6. Cut three lengths of white stamen 'stalks' and curl one end of each by scraping the blade of a pair of scissors along it. Dip the straight ends of these stamens into egg white and then insert them into the centre of the carnation.

PANSY

EQUIPMENT
modelling paste (page 14)
anger tool
covered florist wire
egg white
flower pattern (page 158)
ball tool
paintbrush
food colouring
royal icing
small writing tube

1. Form the calyx first by rolling a piece of green modelling paste, the size of a large pea, into a ball.

2. Hollow out the ball with an anger tool or thick knitting needle, then thin it by pressing it between your thumb and middle finger.

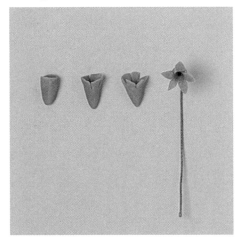

3. Cut the edges of this cup-shape into five and cut each piece into a sharp petal shape. Dip a piece of covered florist wire, bent into a closed hook at one end, into egg white and slip it through the calyx. Curve the wire slightly at the calyx. Allow this to dry thoroughly.

> **NOTE:** When making pansies, it is a good idea to make the calyxes well in advance.

4. Decide on the colour of your pansy, and roll out the modelling paste thinly.

5. Cut out five petals as per the pattern given – two of Shape A, two of Shape B and one of Shape C. Mark with veins by pressing them between your palms.

6. Flute the round edges of each petal slightly with a ball tool, then put them aside to set. Stick the petals, which should

still be pliable, into the calyx with egg white. First the top two petals (Shape A) of the pansy, the left one slightly overlapping the right one.

7. Now add the next two matching petals (Shape B) just over the lower edges of the first two. Lastly, attach the single petal (Shape C) to the calyx so that it just touches the last two petals. Set aside to dry, propping up the petals with sponge or cotton wool if necessary.

8. When all five petals are dry, paint the centre of the pansy with violet to which a little red has been added.

9. Paint the two smaller petals from the narrow part to about the halfway mark with the same colour. With white royal icing in a small writing tube, pipe a small crescent shape on the lower edge of the centre opening and then an inverted 'V' at the top of the opening. When this is dry, paint the crescent shape a deep yellow.

LARGE DAISY

INGREDIENTS
modelling clay*
modelling paste (page 14)
covered florist wire
8-petal daisy cutter or pattern (page 159)
ball tool
pin
tulle

1. If possible, make a mould of the base of a real daisy from modelling clay and bake it according to the directions on the packet until it is hard.

2. Push a piece of green modelling paste, the size of a pea, into the mould. Insert a piece of covered wire, with one end bent over, into the modelling paste. Remove the base from the mould and set it aside to dry.

3. Roll out the modelling paste and cut out two daisies with the daisy cutter.

4. Widen each petal slightly by running a small ball tool gently along each petal.

5. Mark lines along the petals with a pin and hollow the centre of each daisy shape with a ball tool.

6. Wet the centre of one daisy and place the other on top, so positioning the upper petals that they cover the spaces below.

7. Press a small ball of deep golden yellow modelling paste against a piece of tulle to mark it.

8. Wet the inside of the green daisy base made in Step 2 and attach the daisy to it.

9. Attach the centre to the flower and place the daisy on a flower stand to dry.

HALF-OPEN FLOWERS
1. Roll out yellow modelling paste and cut out one daisy with an 8-petal daisy cutter.

2. Widen each petal slightly by running a small ball tool along its length.

3. Mark lines along the petals with a pin.

4. Pinch the centre and set aside while making the green base. Immediately insert the petals into the green base, pressing the base around the petals.

> **NOTE:** Modelling clay is available from hobby shops.

BUD
1. Make a mould of the base of a daisy from modelling clay. Bake until hard. Push a piece of green modelling paste, the size of a pea, into the mould. Insert a piece of covered wire, with one end bent over, into the modelling paste. Remove the paste from the mould, mark with lines and round the top of the base slightly to form a bud.

LEAF
1. Press a real daisy leaf onto modelling clay and bake it according to the directions on the packet until it is hard.

2. Roll out green modelling paste and cut out the daisy leaves, pressing each one onto the mould to vein it. Set the leaves aside to dry slightly curved.

FRANGIPANI

EQUIPMENT
modelling paste (page 14)
frangipani cutter or pattern (page 159)
paintbrush
wooden spoon
egg white
flower stand (or a bottle with a narrow neck)
covered florist wire (optional)
lemon brush-on powder
leaf veiner

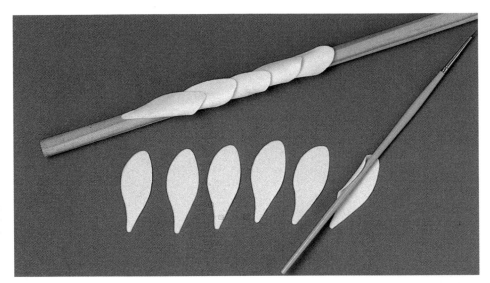

1. Roll out a small piece of white paste (or the colour of your choice) and cut out five petals using a frangipani cutter or pattern. Pick up one petal with a painting knife and cover the other four with plastic. Hold the petal in your left hand between thumb and forefinger. Roll the edge of the petal over the handle of a paintbrush.

2. Place the petal with the rolled edge lengthwise over the handle of a wooden spoon to curve the petal. Prepare the other four petals in the same way and place each one over the narrow part of the previous one to prevent it drying out too quickly. Leave the last petal to dry for a few minutes.

3. Place the first petal, which should still be pliable, in your left hand and paint a little egg white on its lower right-hand edge. Put the second petal onto the edge of the first one and paint its right-hand edge in turn with egg white. Continue in this way, adding all the petals to form a fan.

4. After painting egg white on the right-hand edge of the last petal, roll the petals and join them together to form a cylinder.

5. Press the base of the petals together and twist them slightly. If necessary, cut off any excess paste at their base.

6. Place the flower in a hole in a wooden flower stand. Using the back of your paintbrush and your fingers, gently space the petals evenly and curve them slightly outwards. For variety, some flowers may be left slightly more closed.

7. If desired, a wire stem may be added by pushing it through the centre.

8. Add cornflour to a small amount of lemon brush-on powder to tone it down and brush the centre of the flower.

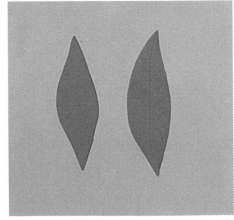

BUD
Roll a piece of modelling paste into a ball the size of a very large pea. Roll this ball into a cylinder that is tapered slightly at each end. Use a knife or pair of scissors to mark four or five lines along the length of the cylinder. Finally, twist the cylinder slightly so that the lines appear to curve around it. Attach a wire stem, if desired.

LEAF
The real frangipani leaf is very large compared with the flower, but in cake decorating the leaf is made smaller than life-size and is cut free-hand. Mark the veins on the leaf with a hatpin or leaf veiner and set it aside to dry.

CYMBIDIUM ORCHID

EQUIPMENT
modelling paste (page 14)
curved modelling tool
brush-on powder
paintbrush
food colouring
anger tool
flower cutter or pattern (page 159)
ball tool
orchid former
egg white
leaf veiner

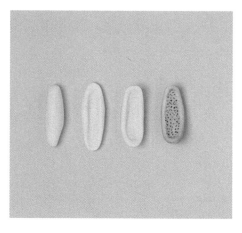

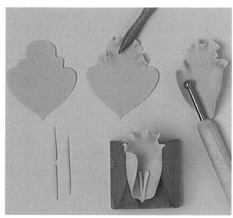

1. Roll a small piece of white modelling paste, twice the size of a large pea, into a cylinder about 15 mm long with rounded ends. Using a curved modelling tool, or the back of a paintbrush, press a hollow into its length and then curve the cylinder slightly. Brush with brush-on powder to match the shade of the petals. Paint tiny dots on the inside curve and set it aside to dry.

2. Roll out modelling paste in the colour of your choice to form the trumpet or lip. Leave the paste slightly thicker where the rounded part of the lip will be when it is cut. Cut out the trumpet and flute along the centre curved portion using an anger tool, then hollow the side sections slightly with a ball tool. Place the trumpet or lip onto an orchid former to dry in the required shape, pulling the centre section downwards. Colour the trumpet or lip with brush-on powder if desired.

3. With yellow modelling paste, roll two very thin cylinders about 2 mm thick and 10 mm long, each one tapering to a point. Attach the cylinders to the trumpet or lip with a little egg white.

4. Cut out five petals from the same colour modelling paste used for the trumpet, using a flower cutter or a pattern. Use a leaf veiner to mark the petals with fine lines. Run a ball tool along the edges of each one to refine them. Colour the petals with brush-on powder if desired then place the petals over a curved shape.

5. Grease a hollow mould and add a ball of paste the size of a large pea. Flatten it, paint it with egg white and then attach the petals and trumpet to create an orchid as shown.

Piping Jelly

Piping Jelly is a most effective medium on cakes and can be used most successfully on butter icing, royal icing, rice paper, plastic icing and on its own. Piping jelly is available in red, green, yellow, neutral and clear, although other colours can be created successfully with the addition of food colouring. It is used in a paper cone with a sharp point or in a cone with a tube.

To show the versatility of this medium, the designs have all been executed on cake boards covered with plastic icing.

1. Pipe the design onto a piece of glass or extruded acrylic with royal icing and a No. 0 writing tube. Allow to dry. Cover the cake board with plastic icing and immediately press the glass stencil into the icing.

2. Colour some piping jelly with food colouring (or with coloured royal icing in equal parts of piping jelly and icing). Put the piping jelly into a small paper cone without a tube and cut off the tip to make a hole the size of a No. 2 writing tube.

3. Have a small paintbrush handy (preferably a flat one 3 or 4 mm wide).

4. Pipe the jelly all around the edge of the design and then brush the edge of the piping jelly towards the centre, leaving a raised edge. Pipe in berries or dots as required.

5. Pipe shells or stars around the edges of the cake board using royal icing in a star tube.

Cocoa Painting

Cocoa painting is a technique which looks effective and impressive yet is very simple to execute. The secret of cocoa painting is to create a contrast between light and shade.

Work on a pastillage plaque (page 15) or directly onto the plastic icing (page 14) on a cake. Use the appropriate brush size to fit the picture.

1. Trace the picture you want to do onto a piece of tracing paper. Using a soft pencil, go over the design on the back of the paper.

2. Place the picture onto the plaque or cake and gently rub or trace over the lines with a sharp object to transfer the tracing onto the icing.

3. Place three small quantities of cocoa butter, each approximately the size of a large pea, into three hollows of a plastic artist's palette or, use an egg poacher.

4. To the first one add about 5 mℓ cocoa powder. To the next, add a little less cocoa and to the third one even less.

5. Place the artist's palette over a bowl of boiling water and mix the cocoa and cocoa butter together with a cocktail stick or toothpick. You will now have three shades of cocoa for painting.

6. Start with the lightest or medium shade and outline the main features or areas.

7. Gradually deepen the shading on the picture, completing it by using the darkest shade of cocoa to contrast the lighter or 'white' areas.

8. Should the cocoa butter mixture harden, making it difficult to paint, re-heat it over a bowl of boiling water.

Wafer Painting

This is a fun technique using rice paper, piping jelly and food colouring. Here are a few points to remember when working with this technique:

1. Use a non-toxic fibre-tip pen to trace the picture onto the *smooth* side of the rice paper.

2. Hold the pen upright and press *very, very* lightly. Avoid thick, heavy lines as these smudge when painting.

3. Use clear piping jelly for the preparation coat or, if not available, a neutral piping jelly can be used. This may have a yellowish tinge, but as it is applied very thinly, it will not spoil the effect.

4. Use a brush with firm, short bristles to apply the gel thinly and evenly over the entire picture, using strokes all in the same direction — from top to bottom or left to right.

5. Remember that the purpose of applying the gel is to protect the rice paper from any moisture. Any unprotected area will disintegrate when water touches it.

6. Colour the picture by using very little water on your brush, mixed with a small quantity of food colouring on a palette. Touch your brush onto a piece of paper towel to remove any excess water. Allow the picture to dry thoroughly.

7. Place the picture face down onto waxed paper and paint the back (rough side) with neutral or clear piping jelly or paint piping jelly onto the cake. Position it on the cake while it is still wet, touching it down in places with the back of a paint-brush.

Part Two

Cupids & Ribbons

*Floodwork cupids and modelling paste ribbons
are used to create this romantic engagement cake.*

INGREDIENTS

1 x 250 mm oval cake (page 12)
1 kg white plastic icing (page 14)
pale blue, yellow, pink and green
  modelling paste (page 14)
pale blue, flesh-coloured or coppertone,
  white, brown and yellow royal icing
  (page 14)

MATERIALS AND DECORATIONS

1 x 300 mm oval cake board
half-round crimper
ribbon inserter
pattern for lettering (page 174), cupids
  (page 163), leaves (page 158)
tubes Nos. 0, 1, 3
tracing paper
waxed paper
paper cone
pink brush-on powder
brown and rose-pink food colouring
fine paintbrush
small brush
non-toxic gold powder
little gin, vodka or caramel oil flavouring
straight-edge cutter
flower cutters
ball tool
pin
snail's trail (page 21)

1. Cover the cake and cake board with white plastic icing.

2. Crimp the top edges of the cake immediately with a 20 mm wide half-round crimper.

3. With a ribbon inserter, cut slots 25 mm apart into the icing on the cake board at approximately 50 mm intervals.

4. Roll out pale blue modelling paste and cut eleven 28 x 9 mm lengths of ribbon and insert them into the slots in the icing as shown.

5. Transfer the two names onto the top of the cake by going over the letters with a sharp object. Pipe over the letters with royal icing in a No. 1 writing tube.

6. Trace the cupids onto tracing paper and tape a piece of waxed paper over the tracing. Outline the cupids with flesh-coloured or coppertone royal icing in a No. 0 or 1 writing tube. Flood the cupids with the same shade, following the instructions for Floodwork on page 31, and allow the cupids to dry.

7. Pipe on the wings with soft white royal icing in a plain cone with a sharp point.

8. When the cupids are dry, brush the cheeks with pink brush-on powder and paint on the eyes and mouth, using brown and rose-pink food colouring on a fine paintbrush.

9. Pipe soft brown royal icing onto the heads and brush the icing to form curls.

10. Overline the crimping with pale blue royal icing in a No. 1 writing tube.

11. Mix the gold powder with a little gin, vodka or caramel oil flavouring and paint the tips of the wings with the gold paint.

12. Carefully remove the cupids from the waxed paper and attach them to the top of the cake with royal icing.

13. Roll out pale blue modelling paste and cut out a 9 mm wide ribbon with a straight-edge cutter and arrange it in a bow.

14. Cut out two more lengths of ribbon, cutting a 'V' into the ends.

15. Attach the bow and the ribbons to the cake with royal icing, cutting the one ribbon to look as though the cupid is holding it.

16. Roll out pink, yellow and pale blue modelling paste and cut out small and medium-sized flowers with the flower cutters. Hollow each flower slightly with a small ball tool and pipe a small yellow royal icing dot into each centre. Attach the flowers to the ribbon and beneath the lettering as shown.

17. Roll out green modelling paste and cut out several leaves, veining them with a pin and adding them to the flowers.

18. Pipe a snail's trail around the base of the cake and around the edge of the board with white royal icing in a No. 3 writing tube.

Cherub & Mandolin

The little cherub playing the mandolin creates an unusual theme for this romantic engagement cake.

INGREDIENTS
1 x 250 mm scalloped cake (page 12)
white, flesh-coloured, pale pink, green, yellow and blue modelling paste (page 14)
white royal icing (page 14)
1 kg white plastic icing (page 14)

MATERIALS AND DECORATIONS
1 x 300 mm scalloped gold cake board
patterns for mandolin (page 165), lettering (page 174), rose leaves (page 158)
tubes Nos. 0, 1, 2, 5
paintbrush
non-toxic gold powder
caramel oil or alcohol
mould for cherub's head
cocktail stick
white water-soluble food colouring (powder)
rose-pink and brown food colouring
pink and red brush-on powder
egg white
umbrella-shaped mould
scrolls, shells, snail's trail (page 22)
roses and rosebuds (page 39)
daisy cutter
pin
covered florist wire
net
blue forget-me-nots (page 40)
gum Arabic glaze (page 15)
white ribbon

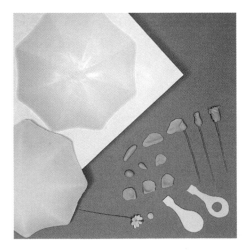

1. Roll out white modelling paste until 2 mm thick and cut out the two shapes for the mandolin. Stick the two pieces together, moulding the edges until they are rounded off.

2. Use royal icing in a No. 0 writing tube to pipe on the strings and fine scrolls. Edge the circle on the mandolin with tiny dots. When completely dry, paint the strings and the scrolls gold using a fine paintbrush. (Mix gold powder with caramel oil or alcohol until it is the correct consistency for painting.)

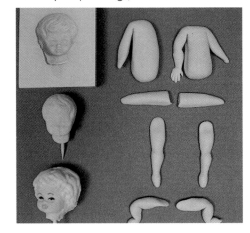

3. Mould the head of the cherub by rolling a piece of flesh-coloured or coppertone modelling paste into a ball and pressing it into the mould. Insert half a cocktail stick into the head and shape and smooth the paste at the back of the head. Allow the head to dry thoroughly.

4. Paint the eyes white and brush the cheeks gently with pink brush-on powder. Paint the lips rose-pink, being careful to keep the mouth small. Paint the eyebrows and the irises brown, leaving a small speck of white for the highlight in each eye, then outline the top of the eye with the same colour.

5. Paint the hair with food colouring or pipe on the hair with royal icing in a No. 2 writing tube. Set the head aside to dry.

6. Roll an elongated piece of paste to form the torso and then cut an arm from each side as shown.

7. Roll and shape the arms gently between your fingers and cut small fingers into the hands. Mark little fingernails on each finger. Position the arms to accommodate the mandolin.

8. Carefully mark the base of the lower back for the baby's bottom. Wet the cocktail stick in the head and insert it into the top of the body.

9. Roll two small pieces of paste, moulding each into a leg and foot and shaping the little toes carefully. Slightly flatten the top of each leg, then attach them to the base of the torso with a little egg white or water and set the cherub aside to dry.

10. Roll out a strip of white modelling paste very thinly and cut a piece which can be draped around the cherub, over each leg and across the front to cross over at the back. Attach the drape at the back with a little egg white.

11. Position the mandolin between the cherub's arms.

12. Roll out a piece of white modelling paste and place it over the umbrella-shaped mould and allow it to dry.

13. When dry, pipe scrolls around the base with white royal icing in No. 2 and No. 1 writing tubes.

14. Pipe scrolls on the cake along the top of each scallop with a No. 2 writing tube. Pipe a small dot at each point.

15. Pipe a small shell border around the base of the cake with a No. 5 star tube.

16. Using the lettering on page 174, trace the two names onto the cake, allowing space for the centre ornament, and pipe over them with a No. 2 writing tube.

17. Make up a number of miniature roses and buds in pale pink modelling paste, following the method used in the photograph.

18. Roll out green modelling paste and cut out a few small rose leaves using the pattern on page 158 as a guide. When the leaves are dry, brush them with a reddish brush-on powder.

19. Roll out white modelling paste and cut out the daisies with a small daisy cutter. Mark lines on each petal with a pin. Bend over the end of a piece of covered wire and then bend the hook over sideways. Thread the straight end of the wire through the centre of the daisy. Roll a tiny piece of yellow modelling paste into a ball and press it against some net to mark it.

Attach it to the centre of the daisy, over the small hook, with a little egg white.

20. Mould tiny blue forget-me-nots, following the instructions on page 40.

21. When all the flowers are dry, paint them with gum Arabic glaze to create a porcelain effect.

22. Attach the umbrella shape to the top of the cake with royal icing, positioning it towards the back of the cake. Pipe a snail's trail all around the base of the umbrella shape with a No. 2 writing tube.

23. Paint the names and all piped scrolls on the cake with gold powder mixed with a little caramel oil or alcohol.

24. Attach the cherub to the top of the umbrella shape with royal icing.

25. Arrange the flowers, leaves and ribbon to form a spray and attach it to the top of the cake with royal icing. Make tiny sprays of flowers and ribbon and attach them to the base of the cake as shown.

Loving Heart

This elegant heart-shaped cake with moulded cream daisies is suitable for any special occasion.

INGREDIENTS
1 x 200 mm heart-shaped cake (page 12)
1 kg white plastic icing (page 14)
red, cream and green modelling paste (page 14)
white royal icing (page 14)

MATERIALS AND DECORATIONS
1 x 250 mm heart-shaped cake board
tracing paper
daisies and leaves (page 43)
pattern for daisy flower and leaf (page 159)
shell border (page 22)
tube No. 5
florist tape
gold ribbon bow (page 35)

 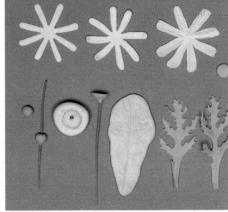

1. Cover the cake with white plastic icing.

2. Make a pattern of a heart by tracing around the cake tin.

3. Using the pattern as a guide, cut out a heart from red modelling paste, to which an equal portion of plastic icing has been added. Cut out the centre of the heart, leaving a frame approximately 25 mm wide. Leave the heart on a smooth flat surface, for example glass, to dry.

4. Following the instructions on page 43, make three cream daisies, three partly-opened flowers and a bud.

5. Make the daisy leaves from green modelling paste, following the instructions on page 43 and using the pattern on page 159 as a guide.

6. Attach the red frame to the top of the cake with royal icing.

7. Pipe a shell border with white royal icing in a No. 5 star tube along the inner and outer edges of the heart and around the base of the cake.

8. Tape the flowers into a spray and attach it to the cake together with a ribbon bow. Attach the leaves to the cake with royal icing.

Lyre & Cupids

Delicately beautiful in pastel shades, this wedding cake features a romantic theme of cupids and flowers.

INGREDIENTS

1 x 300 mm square cake (page 12)
1 x 200 mm square cake
3 kg pale pink plastic icing (page 14)
white pastillage (page 15)
white and pale pink royal icing (page 14)
white, pale and darker pink, blue and
  yellow modelling paste (page 14)

MATERIALS AND DECORATIONS

1 x 350 mm square cake board
1 x 250 mm square cake board
silver braid
glue
pattern for lyre (page 165), lace pieces
  (page 161)
gold sewing thread for strings of lyre
tubes Nos. 1, 2
non-toxic gold powder
gin, vodka or caramel oil flavouring
fine paintbrush
plastic cupid mould
cornflour
pin
waxed paper
pink roses and buds (page 39)
pink brush-on powder
white daisies (page 43)
blue bell-shaped flowers (page 40)
florist tape
cotton wool
pink ribbon bows
shell border (page 22)
100 mm acrylic stand or pillars

1. Cut off the corners of the cakes and the cake boards to create the octagonal shape. Glue fancy silver braid around the edges of the boards.

2. Cover the cakes with pale pink plastic icing, preparing the bottom tier to accommodate the stand or pillars by following the instructions on page 17.

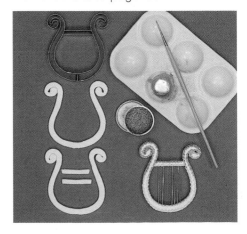

3. Roll out the pastillage to about 2 mm thick and cut out two lyres, using either the pattern or a lyre cutter.

4. Attach the strings to one cross bar and to one half of the lyre with royal icing. Sandwich the lyre together by placing the second cross bar and other half of the lyre on top.

5. Pipe beading around the lyre with royal icing in a No. 1 writing tube and allow to dry thoroughly.

6. Mix the gold powder with a little gin, vodka or caramel oil flavouring and paint the beading, and strings if necessary, using a very fine paintbrush.

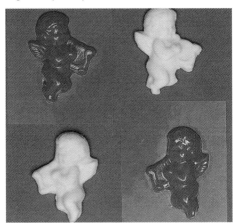

7. Make eight cupids by placing white modelling paste or plastic icing into a cupid mould after first lightly dusting the modelling paste or plastic icing with cornflour. Remove the cupids with a pin and allow them to dry thoroughly.

8. Select a lace piece design on page 161 and pipe the pieces onto waxed paper, following the instructions on page 25, and allow them to dry thoroughly.

9. Mould pale pink roses and darker pink buds from modelling paste, following the instructions on page 39. Brush pink brush-on powder into the centre of each rose.

10. Mould the daisies from white modelling paste following the instructions on page 43.

11. Mould small blue bell-shaped flowers, following the instructions for hyacinths on page 40.

12. Tape the roses, rosebuds and bell-shaped flowers into eight crescent-shaped sprays and attach them to the sides of both cakes with royal icing.

13. Attach the lyre to the top of the cake with royal icing, supporting the lyre with cotton wool until the icing has set.

14. Paint the lyres held by the cupids with gold and attach the cupids to the sides of the cake with royal icing.

15. Make a spray of roses, rosebuds, daisies and bell-shaped flowers and attach it to the top of the cake together with pink ribbon bows.

16. Pipe a shell border around the base of each cake with pale pink royal icing in a No. 2 writing tube.

17. Pipe a 20 mm row of dots with white royal icing and attach the lace pieces at an angle to each cake. Position the pillars or acrylic stand and balance the other tier on top.

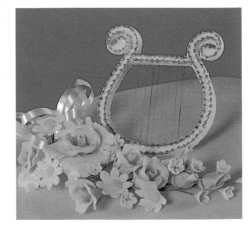

Ornamental Orchids

The pale pink sides visible beneath the extension work, make this an attractive and delicate-looking cake.

INGREDIENTS
1 x 300 mm hexagonal cake (page 12)
1 x 200 mm hexagonal cake
pink and white modelling paste (page 14)
3 kg white plastic icing (page 14)
white royal icing (page 14)

MATERIALS AND DECORATIONS
1 x 375 mm hexagonal cake board
1 x 250 mm hexagonal cake board
patterns for cymbidium orchid petals
   (page 159), embroidery designs
   (page 160), lace pieces (page 161)
cymbidium orchids (page 45)
pink brush-on powder
pink and white hyacinths (page 40)
cornflour
shell border (page 22)
waxed paper
tubes Nos. 0, 1, 2
silver ribbon bows (page 35)
4 x 100 mm pillars or an acrylic stand

1. Mould the orchids from white modelling paste as directed on page 45. Paint the tongue with pink brush-on powder.

2. Mould hyacinths and buds from pink and white modelling paste, following the instructions on page 40.

3. Place the cakes on cake boards and cover the cakes with white plastic icing. Prepare the bottom tier to accommodate the pillars or acrylic stand by following the instructions on page 17.

4. Select an embroidery design from page 160 and make either a glass stencil of the design or pipe it directly onto the cake, using a No. 1 writing tube.

5. Mix pink brush-on powder with a little cornflour to create a pale shade and brush the lower part of the cake sides beneath the embroidery design.

6. Pipe a shell border around the base of each cake with white royal icing in a No. 2 writing tube.

7. Execute the extension work as described on page 26. Using a No. 0 or 1 writing tube, pipe the lace pieces onto waxed paper as described on page 25.

8. Arrange the orchids, hyacinths and ribbon bows into sprays and position them on the top and bottom tiers.

9. Pipe small dots in 20 mm sections with a small writing tube and attach the lace pieces.

10. Position the pillars or acrylic stand on the bottom tier and balance the other tier on top.

Birdbath with Fuchsias

INGREDIENTS
1 x 150 mm round cake (page 12)
1 x 300 mm round cake
burgundy, pink and white modelling
    paste (page 14)
white pastillage (page 15)
white, pale pink and pale green royal
    icing (page 14)
3 kg white plastic icing (page 14)

MATERIALS AND DECORATIONS
1 x 200 mm round cake board
1 x 375 mm round cake board
pattern for birdbath (page 162),
    embroidery design (page 160)
cookie cutter
plastic mould
tubes Nos. 0, 1, 2, 3, 42
piece of glass
non-toxic silver powder
little alcohol or caramel oil
1 x 370 mm circle of expanded styrene,
    25 mm thick and shaped to give the
    effect in the picture
shell border (page 22)
white ribbon bows (page 35)
200 mm acrylic stand

*The centre of this unusual cake
has been cut out and used as the
top tier. The bevel base also adds
to the exclusivity of the design.*

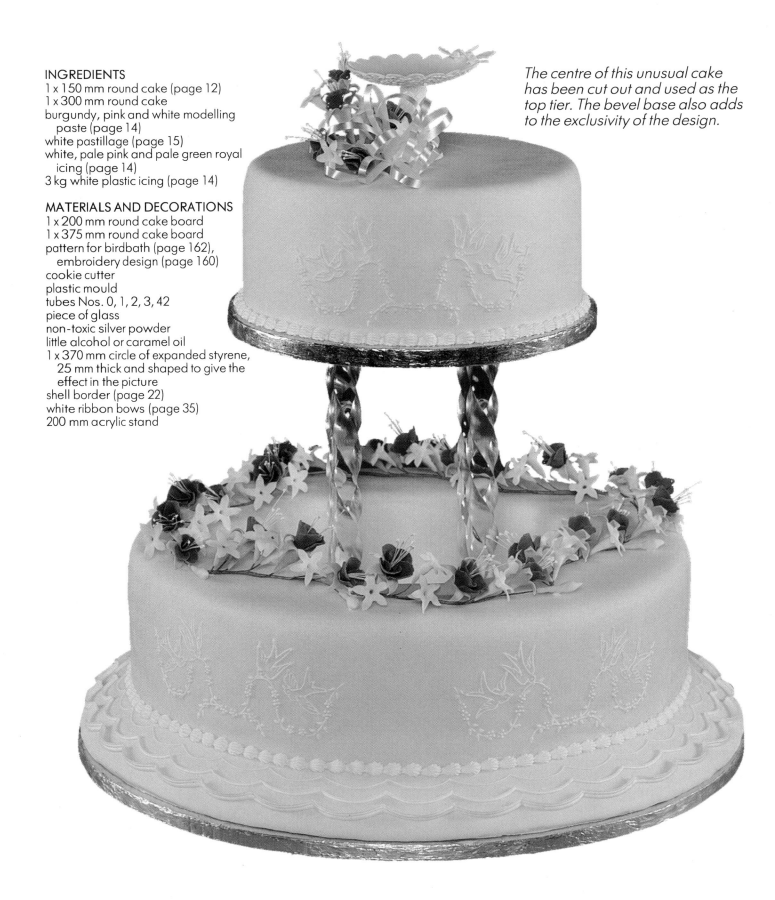

1. Prepare the two cake tins for baking.

2. Place the smaller cake tin in the centre of the larger one. Fill both tins with cake mixture and bake as directed on page 13. This is easier than cutting a circle from the centre of the large cake and will prevent rough edges.

3. Make the small fuchsias from pink and burgundy modelling paste and the jasmine from white paste according to the photographs.

4. Shape white pastillage into a cone shape for the base of the birdbath. Cut out a scalloped circle with a cookie cutter and place it over a plastic mould to form the bath. Allow both to dry.

5. Use a No. 0 writing tube to pipe Cornelli work (page 21) on the outside of the birdbath, leaving a small circle clear in the centre, and on the cone. Attach the top to the base with royal icing and allow it to set and dry thoroughly.

6. Pipe the embroidery design onto a piece of glass with a No. 0 writing tube and royal icing and allow to dry.

7. Using a No. 1 writing tube and royal icing, pipe the wings and tails of the two small birds as shown and allow them to dry. Assemble the birds by piping the bodies and immediately attaching the wings and tails. When the birds are dry, touch the wings with silver powder mixed with a little alcohol or caramel oil.

8. Stick the bevelled styrene to the larger cake board with royal icing and cover it with plastic icing.

9. Roll out the icing for the bottom tier into a large circle and cut a cross in the centre. *The icing must be very pliable and thicker in the centre.* Place the icing over the cake, working quickly to get the icing smooth. Trim away the excess icing in the centre.

10. Place the cake on the covered styrene and immediately press the embroidery design onto the sides of the cake with the glass stencil.

11. Cover the top tier with plastic icing and immediately press the embroidery design onto the sides.

12. Attach the birdbath to the top tier with royal icing and then add the birds.

13. Pipe the embroidery design with a No. 1 writing tube using pale pink royal icing for the embroidered flowers, pale green for the leaves and white for the birds.

14. Pipe a small shell border, preferably with a No. 42 star tube, around the base of each tier and on the inside lower edge of the bottom tier.

15. Mark the positions for the scallops on the bevel by placing three dots immediately above each other and about 10 mm apart. The first dot must be about 10 mm from the top edge. Do the same on the other side of the bevel immediately opposite the first (i.e. at twelve o'clock and six o'clock) and then at the quarter marks (nine o'clock and three o'clock) and so on until the dots are evenly spaced around the bevel and approximately 25 mm apart.

16. Pipe scallops on the bevel, allowing the loops to fall between every two dots. Start with a No. 3 writing tube and white royal icing for the first row of scallops. Pipe a second line over this row with a No. 2 writing tube. Make a second row of scallops using the same tube. With pink royal icing and a No. 1 writing tube, pipe a row of scallops along the top row of dots and then overline the first and second rows of scallops with this pink as well.

17. Tape the fuchsias and jasmine into a garland and place it on top of the larger tier. Tape the remaining flowers and ribbon into a spray for the top tier.

18. Position the acrylic stand in the centre of the bottom tier and balance the other tier on top.

Spring Flowers

With its teardrop-shaped top tier and square bottom tier, this cake is an attractive and pleasing cake for any occasion.

INGREDIENTS

1 x 225 mm teardrop-shaped cake (page 12)
1 x 300 mm square cake
3 kg cream plastic icing (page 14)
orange and yellow royal icing (page 14)
pale lemon, orange and green modelling paste (page 14)

MATERIALS AND DECORATIONS

1 x 260 mm teardrop cake board
1 x 375 mm square cake board
pattern for embroidery design (page 160)
piece of glass
tubes Nos. 0, 1, 2, 42
small shell border (page 22)
miniature daffodil cutter (including a small scalloped cutter)
egg white
covered florist wire
stamens
primrose or primula flower cutter
anger tool
orange brush-on powder
small orange bell-shaped flowers (page 40)
bronze and white ribbon bows
4 x 100 mm pillars or an acrylic stand

1. Pipe the embroidery design of your choice onto a piece of glass with royal icing in a No. 0 writing tube and allow it to dry.

2. Place the cakes on the cake boards and cover the cakes with cream plastic icing. Immediately press the glass stencil onto the sides of the cakes. Prepare the bottom tier to accommodate the pillars or acrylic stand by following the instructions on page 17.

3. Using a No. 1 writing tube and royal icing follow the imprint of the embroidery design in yellow and orange.

4. Pipe a small shell border around the base of each cake with a No. 42 star tube and yellow icing.

5. Make the daffodils by moulding yellow modelling paste into a bell-shape and then cutting the edges with the scalloped cutter.

6. Roll out yellow modelling paste and cut out the six-petal shape and attach the scalloped-edge cup to this with egg white or water. Thread a piece of covered wire through both parts, first bending the wire over at one end.

7. Add a few ready-made stamens or pipe some into the cup-shape using a No. 1 writing tube and yellow royal icing.

8. Make the primroses by moulding a small 'Mexican' hat out of pale lemon modelling paste. Cut out the flower with the primula or primrose cutter.

9. Hollow the centre slightly with an anger tool and thread covered wire into the flower. Allow it to dry.

10. Brush the centre of the primrose with orange brush-on powder.

11. Make the buds by rolling lemon yellow modelling paste into a ball. Roll out green modelling paste and cut out the calyx. Wrap the calyx around the ball and thread a piece of covered florist wire through the calyx and bud.

12. Use orange modelling paste to mould the bell-shaped flowers, following the instructions for making hyacinths on page 40. Attach the flowers to covered florist wire and set them aside to dry thoroughly.

13. Tape the dry flowers and ribbon bows together into small and large sprays and position them on the cakes as shown.

14. Position the pillars or acrylic stand on the bottom tier and place the other tier on top.

Wedding Bell

This lavender-coloured wedding cake incorporates two simple techniques: floodwork and sugar moulding.

INGREDIENTS

1 x 300 x 250 mm oval cake (page 12)
royal icing (page 14)
moulding sugar (page 36)
1,5 kg lavender plastic icing (page 14)
pale pink, lavender and white modelling
    paste (page 14)

MATERIALS AND DECORATIONS

1 x 350 x 300 mm oval cake board
pattern for bell, bride and groom
    (page 172), embroidery bell design
    (page 162), lace pieces (page 161)
plastic mould for bell
food colouring in assorted colours
paintbrush
piece of glass
tubes Nos. 0, 1, 42
ribbon inserter
9 mm wide lavender ribbon
waxed paper
miniature pale pink roses and buds
    (page 39)
small white and lavender bell-type
    flowers (page 40)
lavender ribbon bows (page 35)
shell border (page 22)

1. Flood the picture of the bride and groom with royal icing, following the instructions for Floodwork on page 31. Allow the picture to dry.

2. Fill a plastic bell mould with moulding sugar, packing it in firmly and immediately turning it out. If you are unable to obtain the mould, trace the outline given on page 172 and make the bell in modelling paste or plastic icing, cutting out the inner shape to accommodate the bride and groom. Allow the bell to dry thoroughly.

3. Paint the bride and groom according to the photograph and allow them to dry.

4. Attach the floodwork design to the sugar bell with royal icing and allow to set.

5. Pipe the embroidery design onto a piece of glass with royal icing in a No. 0 writing tube and allow it to dry.

6. Place the cake on the cake board and cover the cake with the lavender plastic icing. Immediately press the glass stencil onto the sides of the cake.

7. Cut slots in the icing with a ribbon inserter, following the instructions for Ribbon insertion on page 36.

8. Cut the lavender ribbon into 30 mm lengths and insert them into the slots as shown.

9. Follow the embroidery design with a No. 1 writing tube and white royal icing and allow it to dry.

10. Position the bell on top of the cake, attaching it with royal icing.

11. Pipe the lace pieces onto waxed paper with a No. 0 or 1 writing tube and white royal icing and set them aside to dry.

12. Make up miniature roses and rosebuds from pale pink modelling paste, following the instructions on page 39. Mould small filler flowers from white and lavender modelling paste as described on page 41. Arrange the flowers and lavender ribbon bows into a spray and position it on top of the cake.

13. Trim the bell with royal icing in a No. 1 writing tube and pipe shells (one up and one down) around the base of the cake with a No. 42 star tube.

14. Attach the lace pieces to the cake following the instructions on page 25.

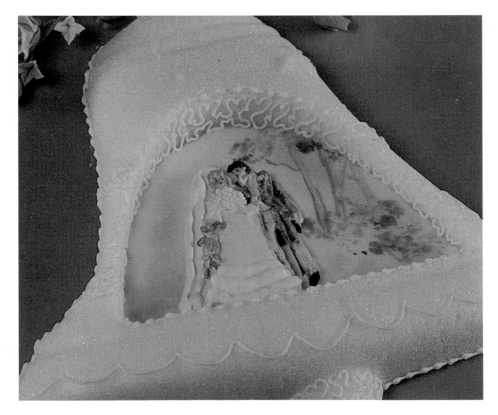

Orange Blossoms

The pale green icing and dainty orange blossoms make this an unusual wedding cake.

INGREDIENTS
1 x 200 mm hexagonal cake (page 12)
1 x 300 mm hexagonal cake
white modelling paste (page 14)
3 kg pale green plastic icing (page 14)
white, green and yellow royal icing
  (page 14)

MATERIALS AND DECORATIONS
1 x 250 mm hexagonal cake board
1 x 350 mm hexagonal cake board
patterns for hearts (page 161), orange
  blossoms (page 158), lace pieces
  (page 161)
waxed paper
tubes Nos. 0, 2
flower cutter
anger tool
pale yellow brush-on powder
stamens
florist wire
yellow ribbon bows
snail's trail (page 21)
4 x 100 mm pillars or an acrylic stand

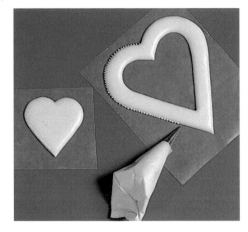

1. Flood the large heart (Shape C) and six smaller hearts (Shape B) on waxed paper with white royal icing according to the instructions on page 31 and allow them to dry.

2. Before removing the hearts from the waxed paper, pipe tiny yellow dots along the edges with royal icing in a No. 0 writing tube.

3. Make the orange blossoms by moulding a 'hat-shape' with white modelling paste and cutting the edges with a flower cutter. Hollow the flowers slightly with an anger tool and dust the centre of each flower with pale yellow brush-on powder.

4. Cut off the ends of the stamens and use only the 'stalks'. Wet the ends of the 'stalks' and insert them into the flower.

5. Roll white modelling paste into oval shapes to form the buds and attach them to pieces of florist wire.

6. Arrange the flowers, buds and yellow ribbon bows into six sprays.

7. Pipe the lace designs onto waxed paper and leave them to dry.

8. Cover the cakes with pale green plastic icing and prepare the bottom tier to accommodate the pillars or acrylic stand by following the instructions on page 17.

9. Pipe a snail's trail around the base of each cake with green royal icing in a No. 2 writing tube.

10. Attach a small ball of white plastic icing to the centre of the top tier with a little royal icing and insert the point of the large heart into the plastic icing. Support the heart until the icing is dry.

11. Arrange the remaining orange blossoms, buds and ribbon bows into a posy around the large heart.

12. Attach two orange blossoms to the large heart with a little royal icing.

13. Attach the flower sprays and small hearts to the sides of the cakes with royal icing.

14. Attach the lace pieces at an angle all around the base of each tier.

15. Position the pillars or acrylic stand on the bottom tier and balance the other tier on top.

Carnation Cascade

The unusual shape, apricot carnations, cream hyacinths and white forget-me-nots make this an appealing wedding cake.

INGREDIENTS
1 x 200 mm square cake (page 12)
1 x 300 mm square cake
3 kg white plastic icing (page 14)
apricot, white and cream modelling paste
 (page 14)
white royal icing (page 14)

MATERIALS AND DECORATIONS
1 x 250 mm cloverleaf cake board
1 x 375 mm cloverleaf cake board
pattern for cloverleaf-shape (page 173)
apricot carnations (page 41)
white forget-me-nots (page 40)
cream hyacinths (page 40)
covered florist wire
pull-up shells and loops (page 22)
tubes Nos. 1, 8
white ribbon bows (page 35)
4 x 100 mm pillars or an acrylic stand

1. Cut each cake into a cloverleaf shape using the pattern on page 173 as a guide.

2. Place the cakes on the cake boards and cover each one with white plastic icing. Prepare the bottom tier to accommodate the pillars or acrylic stand by following the instructions on page 17.

3. Make the carnations, forget-me-nots and hyacinths by following the instructions on the relevant pages.

4. Pipe pull-up shells around the base of each cake with a No. 8 star tube and white royal icing.

5. Pipe loops with a No. 1 writing tube and white royal icing to complete the cake.

6. Make up 16 small sprays of flowers and ribbon bows and attach them to the sides of both tiers with royal icing.

7. Arrange the flowers on a ball of plastic icing in the centre of the top tier to form a posy.

8. Position the pillars or acrylic stand on the bottom tier. Make up a larger spray of flowers and ribbon bows and attach it to the centre of the bottom tier with royal icing. Place the smaller tier on top.

Fountain Fantasy

Although a spectacular effect is created with the addition of a fountain, this design can also be used as a two-tier cake with pleasing results.

INGREDIENTS
1 x 200 mm round cake (page 12)
1 x 300 mm round cake
2 kg white plastic icing (page 14)
white modelling paste (page 14)
white royal icing (page 14)

MATERIALS AND DECORATIONS
1 x 250 mm round cake board
1 x 350 mm round cake board
1 x 400 mm round cake board
cymbidium orchids (page 45)
pink brush-on powder
cornflour
pink food colouring
paintbrush
white hyacinths (page 40)
shell border (page 22)
tube No. 7
fountain (optional)
4 x 350 mm acrylic stand
pink ribbon bows (page 35)
4 x 150 mm pillars or an acrylic stand

1. Place the cakes on the cake boards and cover the cakes with white plastic icing. Prepare the bottom tier to accommodate the pillars or acrylic stand by following the instructions on page 17.

2. Make the orchids in white modelling paste, following the instructions on page 45. When dry, shade the tongue (or trumpet) with pink brush-on powder and paint on tiny pink dots.

3. Make the hyacinths in white modelling paste according to the instructions on page 40. When the flowers are dry, brush the tips of the petals with pink brush-on powder mixed with a little cornflour.

4. Shade the lower half of each cake with pale pink brush-on powder and then pipe a shell border around the base of each cake with royal icing and a No. 7 star tube.

5. Place the fountain and the 350 mm acrylic stand on the large cake board.

6. Arrange a wreath of orchids, hyacinths and ribbon bows on the bottom tier. Make a posy of flowers and ribbon bows on the top tier. Place orchids and ribbon bows around the fountain.

7. Balance the bottom tier on the 350 mm acrylic stand and place the 150 mm pillars or acrylic stand in position on the bottom tier, then balance the other tier on top.

Rosebuds & Butterflies

This exquisite cake lends itself to many attractive ideas for table decorations and gifts for guests at a wedding.

INGREDIENTS
1 x 200 mm round cake (page 12)
1 x 300 mm round cake
3 kg white plastic icing (page 14)
white pastillage (page 15)
white and pale pink modelling paste
    (page 14)
white royal icing (page 14)

MATERIALS AND DECORATIONS
1 x 250 mm round cake board
1 x 350 mm round cake board
1 x 400 mm round cake board
fancy silver edging for boards
snail's trail (page 21)
tubes Nos. 1, 3
paper
pin
small white roses (page 39)
pink brush-on powder
cornflour
pale pink hyacinths (page 40)
small flower cutter
red-tipped stamens (dip tips of white
    stamens in red or pink food colouring)
fuse wire
pattern and stencil for butterfly wings
    (page 162)
cardboard
waxed paper
18 fine black stamens for feelers
sponge or cotton wool
plastic mould for shell
straight-edge cutter or hobby knife
4 x 100 mm pillars or an acrylic stand

1. Cover each board with white plastic icing and cut out a circle the size of each cake from the centre of the two smaller boards. Cut a circle out of the largest board the size of the medium-sized board.

2. Cover the cakes with white plastic icing and position the cakes on the cake boards and the medium-sized cake board on the largest board. Trim each board with fancy silver edging.

3. Prepare the bottom tier to accommodate the pillars or acrylic stand by following the instructions on page 17. Pipe a snail's trail around the base of each cake with white royal icing in a No. 1 writing tube.

4. Cut out two paper circles 200 mm and 300 mm in diameter respectively. Divide each circle into eight equal parts and mark the eight points around the outer edge of each cake with a pin.

5. Use the two smallest sizes of rose petals and make the roses with white modelling paste, following the instructions on page 39. Brush the centres of the roses with pink brush-on powder and the tips with pale pink powder. (Add a little cornflour to make a paler shade.)

6. Make the hyacinths with pale pink modelling paste following the instructions on page 40.

7. Attach a few red-tipped stamens to fuse wire. Using white modelling paste, cut out the blossoms with a flower cutter and hollow them slightly. Brush the blossoms with pink brush-on powder (see photograph on page 76 for the Wishing well cake). Thread the wire through the centre of the flower.

8. Roll out white modelling paste or pastillage very thinly and cut out the butterfly wings to make left and right wings.

9. Cut out a stencil from a thin piece of cardboard. When the wings are dry, place the stencil against each wing and brush dry pink powder onto the exposed part to give it a scalloped edge. Turn the wings over and brush a little pink powder onto the wing where it will meet the body.

10. Pipe the body and head onto a piece of waxed paper with white royal icing in a No. 3 writing tube. Position the wings and the feelers (fine black stamens) into the royal icing while it is still wet. Support the wings with sponge or cotton wool until the body is thoroughly dry.

11. Make the shell by rolling out a piece of white pastillage and placing it into a clear plastic mould that has been dusted with a little cornflour. Keep tipping the pastillage shell out of the mould to ensure that it does not stick. When it has set sufficiently to hold its shape, remove the shell from the mould and allow it to dry.

12. Place a small piece of plastic icing in the shell and arrange the flowers so that they fill the shell.

13. Roll out white modelling paste very thinly and cut out 6 mm wide ribbons with a straight-edge cutter or hobby knife. A tracing wheel or comb may be used to edge the ribbon to give a more realistic finish. For the bows, cut a V-shape into each ribbon end.

14. Use two lengths of ribbon and attach two ends to the moulded shell with royal icing. Position the shell on top of the cake, attaching it with royal icing. Raise the ribbons and support them over a piece of sponge or folded cardboard, allowing the loose ends to rest on the cake thus forming a support for the butterfly. When thoroughly dry, attach a butterfly to the ribbon with a little royal icing.

15. Drape lengths of ribbon between the eight marked positions on each cake and allow them to dry. Attach a butterfly to each point on the bottom tier with royal icing.

16. Form lengths of ribbon into bows and attach them to the top tier at each alternate point marked and around the base of the bottom tier as shown.

17. Form the flowers into sprays and attach them to the cakes.

18. Place the pillars or acrylic stand in position and balance the other tier on top.

Make a Wish

The combination of yellow and white is used most successfully for this single tier wedding cake.

INGREDIENTS

1 x 250 mm hexagonal cake (page 12)
white pastillage (page 15)
white, pale green and yellow royal icing (page 14)
white modelling paste (page 14)
1 kg white plastic icing (page 14)

MATERIALS AND DECORATIONS

1 x 325 mm hexagonal cake board
patterns for brick design (page 167) well (page 166)
tubes Nos. 1, 42
piece of glass
cardboard
jar
stamens
fuse wire
florist tape
blossom cutter
ball tool
yellow brush-on powder
cornflour
pull-up shells with loops (page 22)
shell border (page 22)
white and yellow ribbon bows (page 35)

3. When the parts are dry, assemble the well with royal icing.

4. Cut short lengths of stamen 'stems' and 100 mm lengths of fuse wire. Attach the stamens to the fuse wire by twisting one end of the wire around five stamens.

5. Cut florist tape into four and with one strip, tape the length of the wire including the twisted wire attaching the stamens.

6. Roll out white modelling paste and cut out the blossoms with a blossom cutter. Hollow the blossoms with a ball tool and brush the centres with yellow brush-on powder toned down with a little cornflour.

7. Push the wire stems through the centres of the flowers and set them aside to dry. Pipe a little green royal icing under the flower to attach it firmly to the stem. Allow to dry thoroughly.

8. Cover the cake with white plastic icing and pipe pull-up shells with white royal icing and a No. 42 star tube around the base of the cake. Pipe the loops with yellow royal icing in a No. 1 writing tube.

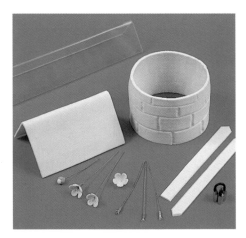

1. Pipe the brick design onto glass with royal icing in a No. 1 writing tube, following the instructions for making a glass stencil on page 28. Allow it to dry.

2. Cut out the parts of the wishing well from pastillage, using the patterns on page 166 as a guide. Immediately press the glass stencil against the sides of the well to mark it. Wrap the base of the well around a jar or tin to form the circular shape. Cover a piece of cardboard, shaped to form the roof, with pastillage and allow all the parts to dry thoroughly.

9. Attach the well to the centre of the cake with royal icing. Pipe a tiny shell border around the base of the well and along the edge of the roof with white royal icing in a No. 42 star tube.

10. Tape the flowers into a large spray and attach it to the wishing well with a yellow and white ribbon bow.

11. Make up seven small flower sprays with ribbon bows and attach one to each corner of the cake and to one side of the well.

A Basket of Roses

This cake, with its flower-filled basket, lace and extension work, is fit for any bride.

INGREDIENTS

1 x 200 mm oval cake (page 12)
1 x 300 mm oval cake
white pastillage (page 15)
white royal icing (page 14)
3 kg white plastic icing (page 14)
green, pink, blue and white modelling paste (page 14)

MATERIALS AND DECORATIONS

1 x 250 mm oval cake board
1 x 375 mm oval cake board
plastic bell for mould
cornflour
patterns for basket (page 162), lace pieces (page 161)
roses (page 39)
white hyacinths (page 40)
blue forget-me-nots (page 40)
shell border (page 22)
tubes Nos. 2, 42
waxed paper
pink and white ribbon bows (page 35)
4 x 100 mm white pillars or an acrylic stand

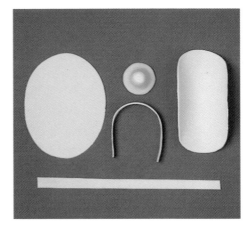

1. Make the stand for the basket by rolling out white pastillage and cutting a circle large enough to go over the plastic bell. Lightly dust the bell with cornflour and press the pastillage firmly over the bell. Move it around every few minutes to prevent the pastillage from sticking to the bell. Remove the pastillage when it can hold its shape.

2. Using the pattern on page 162, cut out an oval for the basket out of white pastillage. Allow it to dry in a slightly curved shape.

3. Cut out a 10 x 230 mm wide strip of pastillage for the handle and allow it to set in a curve to fit the oval base.

4. When all the pieces are dry, attach the curved oval to the bell-shaped base with royal icing and allow it to dry.

5. Attach the handle to the basket with royal icing and support it until it is completely dry.

6. Make the roses, hyacinths and forget-me-nots according to the instructions on pages 39 and 40 and when they are dry, fill the basket with the flowers by pushing them into a small piece of plastic icing. Start with the centre flower and those at either end and on each side, then fill in the gaps with the remaining flowers and ribbon bows.

7. Cover the cakes with white plastic icing and position the basket of flowers on the top tier, attaching it with a little royal icing. Edge the base of the basket with small shells using a No. 42 star tube and white royal icing. Prepare the bottom tier to accommodate the pillars or acrylic stand by following the instructions on page 17.

8. Select a lace piece design and pipe the pieces onto waxed paper, following the instructions on page 25, and allow them to dry thoroughly.

9. Pipe a shell border around the base of each cake with white royal icing in a No. 2 writing tube.

10. Pipe the extension work around the lower half of each cake following the instructions on page 26.

11. Make up small sprays of flowers with ribbon bows and attach them to the cakes with royal icing.

12. Attach the lace pieces to the top edge of the extension work by following the instructions on page 25.

13. Position the pillars or acrylic stand on the bottom tier and balance the other tier on top.

The Bride & Groom

To bring your talents to the fore, attempt this three-tier cake with its lace pieces, extension work, embroidery and moulded figures.

INGREDIENTS

1 x 150 mm square cake (page 12)
1 x 225 mm square cake
1 x 300 mm square cake
4 kg white plastic icing (page 14)
white, red and black modelling paste (page 14)
white and green royal icing (page 14)
flesh-coloured figure moulding paste (page 15)

MATERIALS AND DECORATIONS

1 x 200 mm cake board
1 x 275 mm cake board
1 x 375 mm cake board
pink-tinted blossoms and buds (page 76)
pink brush-on powder
burgundy hyacinths (page 40)
5 x silver ribbon bows
shell border (page 22)
tubes Nos. 0, 1, 2, 3
patterns for embroidery (page 160), lace pieces (page 161), bride's and groom's clothing (page 167)
waxed paper
8 x 100 mm pillars or 2 acrylic stands
male and female plastic figure moulds
tulle
tiny bouquet of flowers

1. Cover the cakes with white plastic icing and prepare the bottom and middle tier to accommodate the pillars or acrylic stands by following the instructions on page 17.

2. Make the blossoms and buds with white modelling paste according to the instructions on page 76 (Steps 4 to 7) and brush the centres of the flowers with pink brush-on powder.

3. Make the hyacinths from burgundy modelling paste according to the instructions on page 40.

4. Combine the blossoms, buds and hyacinths with the ribbon bows to form five sprays.

5. Pipe a shell border around the base of each cake with white royal icing in a No. 2 writing tube.

6. Select an embroidery design from page 160 and make either a glass stencil (page 28) of the design or pipe the design directly onto the cakes with a No. 0 writing tube and white royal icing.

7. Following the instructions on page 26, pipe the extension work onto each cake with royal icing in a No. 3 writing tube.

8. Pipe the lace pieces of your choice onto waxed paper with a No. 1 writing tube and allow them to dry.

9. Attach the lace pieces to all three cakes.

10. Attach the flower sprays to the cake with a little royal icing.

11. Position the pillars or acrylic stands on the cakes and balance the tiers on them.

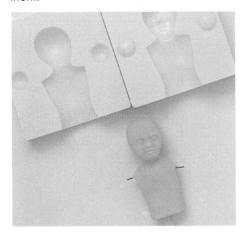

12. Roll pieces of flesh-coloured figure moulding paste into two 'sausages' and thin them, a quarter of the way down where the neck will be, by rolling them between your fingers. Press this paste into the face half of each mould, pressing firmly to ensure clear features.

13. Flatten another two pieces of paste and press them into the torso half of each mould. Press the second half of each mould firmly onto the first to form the head and torso for the bride and groom. Trim away any excess paste and smooth the joins. Remove from the mould and insert half a cocktail stick into each torso and a short piece of covered wire through the shoulders. Allow to dry thoroughly.

14. Brush the cheeks lightly with pale pink brush-on powder. Paint the eyes with white water-soluble food colouring, completing the eye by painting with brown food colouring. Paint the bride's mouth with pink food colouring and the groom's with pink mixed with a touch of brown food colouring. Pipe on the hair with royal icing in a No. 1 or 2 writing tube.

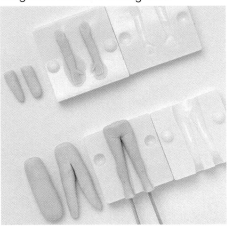

15. Roll two pieces of figure moulding paste into two 'sausages' and then cut them in half as shown. Press the paste into each leg mould and press the second half of the mould firmly on top. Trim away any excess paste and insert a thin skewer into each leg. Immediately attach the torso to the legs by inserting the cocktail stick into the waist. Allow to dry thoroughly.

16. Roll four pieces of flesh-coloured moulding paste into 'sausages' and press each one into an arm mould. Trim away any excess paste and curve the arms as necessary. Press a small hole into each arm to accommodate the wire in the shoulders. Set aside to dry thoroughly.

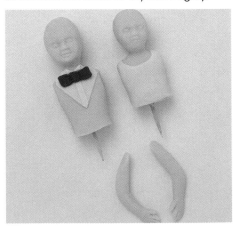

17. Roll out white modelling paste and cut out the bride's clothing, using the patterns on page 167 as a guide. Cover the pieces with plastic to prevent them drying out. Cut out a 140 mm, 80 mm and 40 mm diameter circle from modelling paste. Cut out a 20 mm circle from the middle of the larger and medium circles and a 10 mm circle from the small circle. Frill the edges of each circle slightly with an anger tool.

18. Attach the bodice to the bride by moistening the back and lower edges, then attach the large and medium circle with water or royal icing to form the skirt. Pipe a tiny embroidery design onto the skirt.

19. Attach the sleeves to the arms by moistening all the edges, except the wrists, with water. Cut two small narrow strips from modelling paste, frill them slightly and attach one to each wrist. Attach the arms to the shoulders with royal icing or water. Slit the smaller circle from the outer edge to the centre and attach it to the bodice to form a cape. Gather a piece of tulle and attach it to the head

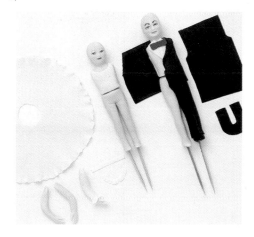

with royal icing to form the veil. Attach a bouquet of tiny flowers to the bride's hands with royal icing.

20. Roll out white, red and black modelling paste and cut out the groom's clothing, using the patterns on page 167 as a guide. Moisten the back and lower edges of the shirt front and attach it to the torso. Attach the shoes to the feet.

21. Form the red modelling paste into a bow tie and attach it to the groom's neck. Attach each trouser leg as shown by moistening the edges. Press a crease into the front of each trouser leg. Attach the jacket and fold over the lapels. Moisten all the edges of the sleeves, except the cuffs, and attach them to the arms. Add a cuff to each wrist and attach the arms to the shoulders with royal icing or water.

22. Position the bride and groom on the top tier, attaching them by pushing the skewers into the cake.

Silver Wedding

The icing on the top tier is brought right over the edge of the cake board to create this impressive two-tier anniversary cake.

INGREDIENTS
1 x 300 mm round cake (page 12)
1 x 200 mm hexagonal cake
3 kg white plastic icing (page 14)
white and yellow royal icing (page 14)
pale and darker pink, green and white modelling paste (page 14)
white pastillage (page 15)

MATERIALS AND DECORATIONS
1 x 375 mm round cake board
1 x 200 mm hexagonal cake board
shell border (page 22)
tubes Nos. 1, 7, 8
pull-up shells and loops (page 22)
pale pink roses and buds (page 39)
pink brush-on powder
white and pink forget-me-nots (page 40)
pink filler flowers (page 40)
patterns for lettering (page 174), rose leaves (page 158), numerals (page 175)
waxed paper
non-toxic silver powder
little gin, vodka or caramel oil flavouring
paintbrush
small flower cutter
sponge
silver ribbon bow

1. Cover the cakes, including the small cake board, with white plastic icing. Place the smaller tier and cake board in the centre of the larger tier.

2. Pipe a shell border around the base of the smaller cake with white royal icing in a No. 7 star tube.

3. Pipe pull-up shells and loops around the base of the bottom tier with white royal icing in a No. 8 star tube and No. 1 writing tube respectively. Pipe two rows of tiny dots above the pull-up shells.

4. Mould roses and buds from pale pink modelling paste, brush the tips of the petals with pink brush-on powder and add green calyxes.

5. Mould small white and pink forget-me-nots and pink filler flowers, following the instructions on page 40.

6. Roll out white pastillage and cut out a 110 x 145 mm rectangle for the scroll.

7. Trace off the lettering and transfer it to the pastillage scroll by going over the letters with a sharp object. Roll the scroll as shown and allow it to dry. Pipe over the imprint with white royal icing.

8. Roll out white modelling paste and cut out the rose leaves. Vein the leaves as shown and allow them to dry.

9. Flood the numerals on a piece of waxed paper, following the instructions for Floodwork on page 31. When dry, attach them to the scroll with royal icing.

10. Mix the silver powder with a little gin, vodka or caramel oil flavouring and paint the lettering, numerals, leaves, the edges of the scroll and the tiny dots around the sides of the cake.

11. Roll out pink modelling paste and cut out the tiny forget-me-nots with the smallest flower cutter. Pipe yellow royal icing into each centre. Attach the flowers in scallops around the edge of each tier with royal icing.

12. Attach the scroll to the top tier with royal icing, supporting it with a sponge until the icing is dry.

13. Form medium-sized sprays with the roses, rosebuds, forget-me-nots, filler flowers and silver leaves and attach them to the bottom tier as shown.

14. Form a larger spray with the flowers and a ribbon bow and attach it to the top tier with royal icing.

Golden Years

Carnations, loops, pull-up shells and forget-me-nots combine to create this elegant cake for a 50th Wedding Anniversary.

INGREDIENTS

1 x 200 mm hexagonal cake (page 12)
750 g white plastic icing (page 14)
white and golden-yellow royal icing (page 14)
white, golden-yellow, orange and green modelling paste (page 14)

MATERIALS AND DECORATIONS

1 x 250 mm hexagonal cake board
pull-up shells (page 22)
tubes Nos. 1, 8
patterns for numerals (page 175), leaves (page 158)
snail's trail (page 21)
non-toxic gold powder
gin, vodka or caramel oil flavouring
fine paintbrush
loops (page 00)
golden-yellow carnations (page 41)
orange forget-me-nots (page 40)
florist tape
golden ribbon bows

1. Cover the cake with plastic icing.

2. Pipe pull-up shells around the base of the cake with white royal icing in a No. 8 star tube.

3. Roll out white modelling paste and cut out the numerals. Attach them to the top of the cake with royal icing. Pipe a snail's trail around the edge of the numerals with golden-yellow royal icing in a No. 1 writing tube. Mix the gold powder with a little gin, vodka or caramel oil flavouring and, when the numerals are dry, paint the edges with gold paint, using a fine paintbrush.

4. Fill a No. 1 writing tube with golden-yellow royal icing and pipe evenly spaced dots along the top edges of the cake. Pipe loops from one dot to the next around the top edge. Pipe a second row, making the loops slightly longer than the first.

5. Pipe an even number of dots in a row above the pull-up shells with golden-yellow royal icing in a No. 1 writing tube and allow them to dry.

6. With royal icing in a No. 1 writing tube, pipe a short and a long loop between the first and third dot, between the second and fourth, third and fifth, and so on all around the cake.

7. Make about 14 small carnations from golden-yellow modelling paste, following the instructions on page 41.

8. Roll out orange modelling paste and cut out 30 forget-me-nots with a blossom cutter. Pipe a dot of yellow icing in the centre of each flower and attach them to the top edge of the cake and at intervals along the base border.

9. Cut out two small leaves and about six larger leaves from green modelling paste. Attach the small leaves to the flower at the base as shown.

10. Tape the carnations into two sprays and attach them to the cake in a crescent shape. Add ribbon bows and leaves, attaching them with royal icing.

Christening Cradle

Decorated with a cradle, flower sprays, ribbons and tiny bootees, this cake is fit for a princess.

INGREDIENTS

1 x 300 mm round cake (page 12)
white pastillage (page 15)
white, pink and yellow royal icing (page 14)
white, pink, blue and pale green modelling paste (page 14)
2 kg pale pink plastic icing (page 14)

MATERIALS AND DECORATIONS

1 x 375 mm round cake board
pattern for cradle (page 171)
cardboard
cornflour
hobby knife
tubes Nos. 00, 0 or 1, 4, 42
non-toxic gold or silver powder
little gin, vodka or caramel oil flavouring
light brown and pink food colouring
fine paintbrush
flower cutter
tulle
piece of ribbon
roses (page 39)
pale pink brush-on powder
hyacinths and forget-me-nots (page 40)
shell border (page 22)
pink ribbon bows (page 35)

1. Trace the pattern for the cradle onto cardboard and cut out the pieces. Use a section of a cardboard paper towel roll as a mould for the cradle base, scoring along the centre to form the right shape.

2. Roll out white pastillage until 2 mm thick on a board lightly dusted with cornflour. Cut out the cradle pieces.

3. Place the pastillage base over the cardboard roll and allow to dry. Curve the top of the headboard slightly about 25 mm from the top. Allow the parts to dry thoroughly. It will take about 72 hours or longer depending on the weather. Remember to turn the pastillage parts over regularly so that they dry more evenly and thoroughly.

4. When totally dry, assemble the cradle with royal icing and edge it with a line of icing and trim with small designs using a small writing tube. When dry, paint the edging and designs with silver or gold powder mixed with a little gin, vodka or caramel oil flavouring.

5. Make a small pillow and blanket with white and pink modelling paste respectively. Decorate as desired.

6. Make the baby's face by rolling a piece of modelling paste into a ball or by piping with royal icing in a No. 4 writing tube. When dry, paint on the features.

7. Following the instructions for Figure Piping on page 35, pipe a large ball of pink royal icing with a No. 4 writing tube and press the baby's face into it. When dry, pipe tiny dots around the edge of the bonnet with a No. 0 or 1 writing tube and white royal icing.

8. Roll out small pieces of white and blue modelling paste and cut out two flowers with a tiny flower cutter. Pipe yellow royal icing into their centres.

9. Cut a piece of tulle approximately 230 x 135 mm and attach it to the headboard with the two tiny flowers and a piece of ribbon.

10. Hand mould the four pairs of bootees from white modelling paste and allow them to dry.

11. Cut out tiny flowers from pink modelling paste and tiny leaves from pale green modelling paste. Trim each bootee with a flower and two leaves.

12. Mould small roses from white modelling paste as described on page 39 and brush the edges of the petals with pale pink brush-on powder.

13. Make blue forget-me-nots and pink hyacinths according to the instructions on page 41.

14. Cover the cake and board with pale pink plastic icing and pipe small shells around the base of the cake and around the edge of the cake board with pale pink royal icing in a No. 42 star tube.

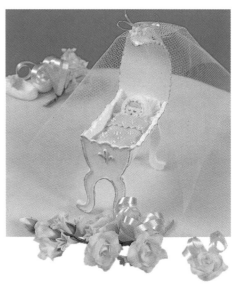

15. Make small sprays of roses, forget-me-nots, hyacinths and pink ribbon bows.

16. Position the cradle, flower sprays and bootees on the cake, attaching them with royal icing.

Sleeping Beauty

Floodwork is effectively combined with modelling paste in pastel shades to create a christening cake with a difference.

INGREDIENTS
1 x 250 mm oval cake (page 12)
1 kg white plastic icing (page 14)
royal icing in assorted pastel shades (page 14)
white, pink, blue and green modelling paste (page 14)

MATERIALS AND DECORATIONS
1 x 300 mm oval cake board
pattern for floodwork picture (page 163), leaves (page 158)
tracing paper
soft pencil
tubes Nos. 0, 1
straight-edge cutter
blue and pink forget-me-nots (page 40)
brown and pink food colouring
fine paintbrush

1. Cover the cake with white plastic icing.

2. Copy the picture on page 163 onto tracing paper and transfer the design to the top of the cake by tracing over the picture with a sharp object.

3. Outline the sections of the picture in the relevant colours with royal icing in a No. 1 writing tube.

4. Flood the picture in sections, following the instructions for Floodwork on page 31, remembering to allow each section to set before flooding an adjacent part.

5. Mould the birds from white modelling paste as shown.

6. Cut 10 mm wide ribbons with a straight-edge cutter from pink modelling paste and place the ribbons and the birds in position on top of the cake, attaching them with royal icing.

7. Cut a 20 mm wide ribbon from pink modelling paste and position it around the base of the cake. Make a bow as shown in the photograph and attach it to the ribbon around the base.

8. Make tiny forget-me-nots from pink and blue modelling paste by following the instructions on page 40.

9. Cut out the leaves from green modelling paste and allow them to dry. Do not let them dry flat as they will look unnatural on the cake.

10. Paint the features onto the faces of the figures in the floodwork picture with food colouring and a fine paintbrush.

11. Trim the cradle and the clothes with pink or blue royal icing in a No. 0 writing tube and attach a small ribbon of pink modelling paste to the cradle.

12. Pipe the child's name onto the top ribbon and the date of birth onto the bottom ribbon with royal icing in a No. 1 writing tube.

13. Attach the flowers and leaves to the cake with royal icing.

The Family Tree

A combination of floodwork, figure piping and moulded work is used to create this unusual christening cake.

INGREDIENTS

1 x 300 x 225 mm rectangular cake
   (page 12)
flesh-coloured, pale pink, brown, white,
   grey, black, green and yellow royal
   icing (page 14)
1,5 kg white plastic icing (page 14)
white, pink and yellow modelling paste
   (page 14)

MATERIALS AND DECORATIONS

1 x 325 x 250 mm rectangular cake board
patterns for floodwork faces, cradle,
   name plates, plaques and tree
   (page 164)
tracing paper
waxed paper
tubes Nos. 0, 1, 2, 4, 7, 42, 101 (Ateco)
food colouring
fine paintbrush
small brush
egg white
plain paper cone
flower cutter
shell border (page 22)

5. Figure pipe the tiny teddy bear in the cradle and the little birds with a No. 0 writing tube and the little bunnies with a No. 2 writing tube, following the instructions for Figure Piping on page 35.

6. Cover the cake with white plastic icing.

7. Trace the tree pattern and transfer the design to the cake by tracing over the design with a sharp object. Fill in the areas with brown royal icing in Nos. 2 and 4 writing tubes. Brush these areas with a small brush to give the rough appearance of bark.

8. Roll out white modelling paste and cut out the name plates and plaques. When they are dry, pipe on the names, 'My Family Tree' and the baby's name and

date of birth with royal icing in a No. 0 writing tube.

9. Pipe a rough line with brown icing underneath the tree, adding tufts of grass with green royal icing in a No. 1 writing tube.

10. Attach the faces, cradle, name plates and plaques to the cake with royal icing.

11. Roll out pink and yellow modelling paste and cut strips to form the ribbons. Attach them to the cradle and to the girl's hair with a little egg white.

12. Fill a plain paper cone with green royal icing. Flatten and cut the end and pipe on the leaves on the tree.

13. Cut out the flowers from modelling paste in assorted colours with a small flower cutter. Pipe a small dot in the centre of each flower with yellow royal icing in a No. 1 writing tube.

14. Place the flowers, birds, teddy and bunnies in position, attaching them with royal icing.

15. Pipe stems and leaves around the sides of the cake and when dry add the flowers.

16. Pipe a shell border around the base of the cake with a No. 7 star tube and a small shell border around the top edge with a No. 42 star tube.

1. Trace each face on page 164 onto tracing paper. Tape a piece of waxed paper on top of the tracing paper and outline the faces with flesh-coloured royal icing in a No. 1 writing tube. Flood the faces, following the instructions for Floodwork on page 31 and allow them to dry thoroughly.

2. Paint on the features with food colouring and a fine paintbrush and pipe on the hair with royal icing in the appropriate colours in a No. 1 writing tube.

3. Trace the picture of the cradle onto tracing paper. Tape a piece of waxed paper on top and outline the cradle and the baby's face with royal icing in a No. 1 writing tube. Flood the picture, remembering to allow each section to dry before flooding the adjacent section.

4. When the cradle is dry, pipe on the frills with pale pink royal icing in a small petal tube (Ateco No. 101 or similar). Trim the pillow and blanket with royal icing in a No. 0 writing tube. Paint on the features with food colouring and add tiny pink dots to the pillow and blanket.

Autumn Wishes

INGREDIENTS

1 x 250 mm round cake (page 12)
1 kg cream plastic icing (page 14)
royal icing (page 14)
cream pastillage (page 15)
brown, blue, orange, yellow, pink, and green modelling paste (page 14)

MATERIALS AND DECORATIONS

1 x 300 mm round cake board
patterns for crazy paving and parts of well (page 166), leaves (page 158)
piece of glass
tubes Nos. 1, 43
piece of cotton
rose petal cutter
egg white
pink, brown, yellow and green brush-on powder
covered florist wire
pull-up shells (page 22)
loops and dots (page 21)

1. Cover the cake with cream plastic icing.

2. Pipe the crazy paving pattern onto glass with a No. 1 writing tube and royal icing and allow it to dry. Cut the parts for the wishing well from cream pastillage and immediately press the glass stencil onto the base of the well. Allow the pieces to dry thoroughly in the desired shapes as described in Step 2 on page 76.

3. Shape the bucket in the wishing well from brown modelling paste.

4. Roll a thin rod of pastillage or modelling paste to fit between the two uprights and allow it to dry. Assemble the well with royal icing, attaching the bucket to the rod with a piece of cotton or thin wire.

5. With a rose petal cutter, cut the tiles for the roof from coloured modelling paste and attach them to the dry roof with egg white.

6. Brush the crazy paving with pink, brown and yellow brush-on powder.

7. Using the leaf pattern, cut out the leaves from green modelling paste and attach them to covered wire stems.

8. Brush the leaves with brown, green and pink brush-on powder to create the autumn shades.

9. Pipe pull-up shells all around the base of the cake with a No. 43 star tube and royal icing. Pipe brown loops with a No. 1 writing tube around the base and loops and dots around the top edge of the cake.

10. Attach the wishing well to the centre of the cake with royal icing.

11. Form a spray with the leaves and attach it to the well with royal icing.

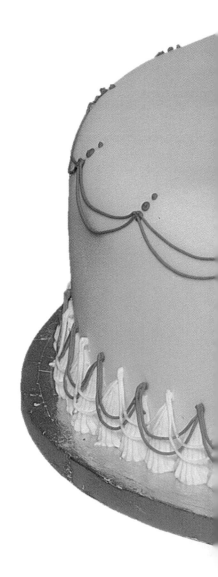

This delightful wishing well with the autumn-coloured leaves makes an appealing decoration on a cake for a man or woman. It can also be used for someone retiring with the addition of the inscription 'Wishing you well on your retirement'.

Graduation Day

*A cake suitable for a young man or woman
to mark that special graduation day.*

INGREDIENTS
1 x 250 mm hexagonal cake (page 12)
1 kg pale blue plastic icing (page 14)
white, red and black modelling paste
   (page 14)
red and white royal icing (page 14)

MATERIALS AND DECORATIONS
1 x 300 mm hexagonal cake board
straight-edge cutter
domed flower nail
tubes Nos. 0, 1, 7 or 8
black food colouring
fine paintbrush
pattern for lettering (page 175)
waxed paper
scrolls (page 22)

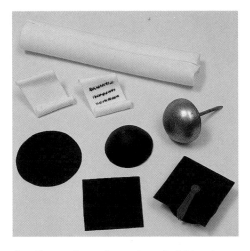

1. Cover the cake with pale blue plastic icing.

2. Roll out a piece of white modelling paste and cut out a 110 x 120 mm rectangle for the diploma. Roll it over a tube or cylinder until it is set. Roll out a piece of red modelling paste and cut a thin strip with a straight-edge cutter to form the ribbon. Place it around the diploma and set it aside to dry.

3. For the mortar boards, roll out black modelling paste and cut out six 50 mm diameter rounds, pressing them onto a dome-shaped flower nail to form the crown. Remove them from the nail and set them aside to dry.

4. Cut out six 50 mm squares and when they are dry, attach the domes to the squares with royal icing. Pipe on the tassles with red royal icing in a No. 1 writing tube.

5. Roll out white modelling paste and cut out six 35 x 65 mm pieces. Shape the certificates according to the photograph and paint them with black food colouring and a fine paintbrush to resemble printing. Set them aside to dry.

6. Using the lettering on page 175, trace 'Congratulations' onto tracing paper and outline each letter with red royal icing in a No. 0 writing tube onto waxed paper. Flood the lettering with red royal icing and when dry, attach the letters to the top of the cake with royal icing.

7. Attach the diploma, mortar boards and certificates with royal icing as shown in the photograph.

8. Pipe scrolls around the base of the cake with white royal icing in a No. 7 or 8 star tube. Pipe red dots at intervals around the base with a No. 1 writing tube.

Hello Sailor

An attractive cake with a naval theme that is ideal for the men in the family.

INGREDIENTS
1 x 250 mm scalloped cake (page 12)
1 kg white plastic icing (page 14)
blue, white and brown royal icing
   (page 14)
white, brown, pale and dark blue
   modelling paste (page 14)

MATERIALS AND DECORATIONS
1 x 300 mm round cake board
tracing paper
patterns for anchor and ship (page 168),
   lettering (page 174)
waxed paper
sticky tape
tubes Nos. 1, 3
pale blue brush-on powder
blue food colouring
paintbrush
rope border (page 28)
snail's trail (page 21)

1. Cover the cake with plastic icing.

2. Make six tracings of the pattern for the anchor. Stick a piece of waxed paper on top of the tracing paper with sticky tape. Outline the anchors with blue royal icing in a No. 1 writing tube and then flood the anchors, following the instructions for Floodwork on page 31.

3. Cut an 85 x 30 mm plaque from modelling paste. Using the lettering on page 174, trace 'DAD' onto the plaque by going over the letters with a sharp object. Outline the letters with blue royal icing and then flood the letters to match the anchors. Outline the plaque with white royal icing in a No. 1 writing tube. Set aside to dry.

4. Transfer the pattern of the ship given on page 168 onto the cake by outlining the design with a sharp object.

5. Cut a 300 mm circle out of tracing paper and cut out a circle from the centre measuring 180 mm in diameter. Place the circle over the centre of the cake and brush the inner circle with pale blue brush-on powder.

6. Use the pattern to cut out the hull from brown modelling paste and attach it to the cake by painting the back of the paste with a little water.

7. Cut out the sails and pennant from pale blue modelling paste and the spinnaker from dark blue modelling paste. Paint stripes on the spinnaker with blue food colouring. Paint the back with water and attach the spinnaker to the cake. Paint the backs of the sails with water and attach them in position on the cake.

8. Pipe the masts with a No. 3 writing tube and the rigging and trimming of the hull with a No. 1 writing tube and brown royal icing.

9. Paint the back of the pennant with water and attach it to the top of the mast.

10. Pipe soft white royal icing to form the clouds and brush them into shape.

11. Pipe soft blue royal icing at the base of the ship to form the sea and add white royal icing to create foam.

12. Pipe a rope border around the picture with blue royal icing and a No. 3 writing tube.

13. Pipe a brown snail's trail around the base of the cake with a No. 3 writing tube.

14. Attach the anchors to the sides of the cake at the point of each scallop with a little royal icing.

15. Once the rope border is dry, position the 'DAD' plaque on the top of the cake with royal icing.

To Mother with Love

The floodwork collar and red roses make this a cake any mother would be delighted to receive.

INGREDIENTS
1 x 200 mm round cake (page 12)
750 g white plastic icing (page 14)
white, red and pale green royal icing
    (page 14)
red and white modelling paste (page 14)

MATERIALS AND DECORATIONS
1 x 275 mm round cake board   .
patterns for floodwork collar and
    embroidery design (page 167),
    lettering (page 175)
greaseproof paper
piece of glass
waxed paper
sticky tape
tubes Nos. 0, 1, 2, 3
beading (page 21)
piped roses (page 34)
moulded roses, half roses and buds
    (page 39)
non-toxic silver powder
little gin, vodka or caramel oil flavouring
shell border (page 22)
silver ribbon bow (page 35)

1. Cover the cake with white plastic icing.

2. Cut a greaseproof paper circle approximately 10 mm smaller all round than the cake board and draw the collar design onto it. .

3. Place the collar design under a piece of glass and stick a square of waxed paper on top of the glass with sticky tape.

4. Outline the collar with a No. 1 writing tube and white royal icing. Now flood the collar, following the instructions for Floodwork on page 31, remembering to flood from alternate sides so that the icing flows together and does not leave join marks. Set it aside to dry thoroughly. It will take approximately 72 hours in warm weather.

5. Cut out a second collar pattern, making it a few millimetres smaller than the first one and remove the centre circle, plus a few extra millimetres, so that the paper

collar fits over the cake and slides down to the board.

6. Pipe a line around the paper collar on the board with royal icing in a No. 1 writing tube. Remove the paper and flood the collar shape on the board as described above. Allow this to dry.

7. Pipe beading around the edge of both collars with white royal icing in a No. 1 writing tube.

8. Pipe eight small roses with red royal icing, following the instructions on page 34. Mould three large roses, three half roses and a bud from red modelling paste, following the instructions given on page 39.

9. Pipe the embroidery design onto both collars and onto the sides of the cake. Follow the design with the relevant colours in a No. 0 or 1 writing tube. Attach the small piped roses to the collars with royal icing.

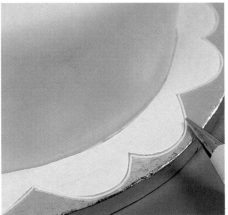

Step 5

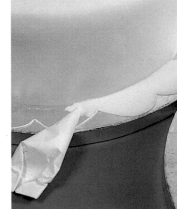

Step 6

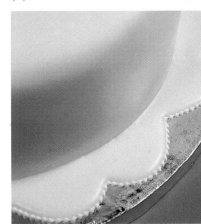

Step 7

Step 12

Step 13

Step 14

10. Place the paper collar pattern on top of the cake and prick a circle onto the cake approximately 3 mm larger than the centre circle.

11. Trace 'Mother' on page 175 onto a 50 x 100 mm piece of white modelling paste. Outline the letters with royal icing in a No. 1 writing tube and then flood them, following the instructions for Floodwork on page 31, and allow them to dry thoroughly.

12. Paint the letters silver by mixing the silver powder with a little alcohol or caramel oil flavouring. Attach the plaque to the cake with royal icing. Pipe a shell or beading border around the plaque with a No. 2 writing tube.

13. Carefully remove the paper from the top collar by pulling the paper over the edge of the table while supporting the collar. Turn the collar around to release the other half.

14. Pipe a line of royal icing with a No. 3 writing tube, following the pinpricks to form a circle. Attach the collar to the cake by placing it onto the royal icing circle.

15. With a No. 1 or 2 writing tube, pipe a small shell or beading border between the cake and the collar to neaten the join.

16. Attach the spray of larger roses and rosebuds with a silver ribbon bow to the top of the cake.

My Valentine

Ribbon insertion, loops, picot edging and blossoms combine to create this simple yet attractive design.

INGREDIENTS
1 x 160 x 200 mm oval cake (page 12)
750 g white plastic icing (page 14)
pink, white, blue and green modelling
    paste (page 14)
white and yellow royal icing (page 14)

MATERIALS AND DECORATIONS
1 x 250 x 210 mm oval cake board
piece of paper
10 mm wide ribbon
ribbon inserter
patterns for heart (page 161) leaves
    (page 158)
ball tool
picot edging (page 24)
tubes Nos. 00, 0, 1, 5, 42
shell border (page 22)
straight-edge cutter
frill ruler
anger tool
medium and small flower cutters

1. Cut a paper pattern the shape of the cake and mark the slots for the ribbon approximately 10 mm and 25 mm apart.

2. Cut the ribbon into 12 mm lengths, reserving some for the bow.

3. Cover the cake with white plastic icing and immediately cut the slots into the top of the cake with a ribbon inserter, using the pattern as a guide. Insert the ribbon.

4. Roll out a piece of pink modelling paste to 2 or 3 mm thick and cut out the heart (Shape A) on page 161.

5. Run a ball tool round the edge of the heart to smooth and round it slightly.

6. Attach the heart to the top of the cake with water, egg white or royal icing.

7. Pipe a lace design, made up of loops and picot edging, around the heart with white royal icing in a No. 0 writing tube.

8. Embroider small flowers in the spaces between the ribbon insertion with white royal icing in a No. 00 or 0 writing tube.

9. Pipe a shell border around the base of the cake with royal icing in a No. 5 star tube.

10. Roll out white modelling paste and cut a strip, approximately 20 mm wide and long enough to go around the cake, cutting one edge with a straight-edge cutter and the other with a frill ruler. Frill this edge with an anger tool.

11. Pipe royal icing onto the back of the frill along the straight edge and attach the frill to the shells.

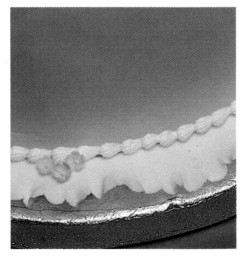

12. Pipe a small shell border around the base of the cake, above the frill, with white royal icing in a No. 42 star tube.

13. Pipe 'Be Mine' onto the heart with white royal icing in a No. 1 writing tube.

14. Roll out pink, blue and green modelling paste and cut out the blossoms and leaves. Pipe a dot of yellow icing into the centre of each blossom and attach the blossoms and leaves to the heart, to the frill and to the side of the cake with royal icing.

15. Attach a bow to the top of the cake with a little royal icing.

Brimful of Blossoms

Roses and hyacinths encircle this pretty, feminine hat — a perfect cake to celebrate Mother's Day.

INGREDIENTS
1 x 150 mm round cake (page 12)
1 kg pale egg-yellow plastic icing (page 14)
pale apricot and white modelling paste (page 14)
white royal icing (page 14)

MATERIALS AND DECORATIONS
1 x 300 mm round cake board
cotton wool
roses (page 39)
hyacinths (page 40)
4 gold ribbon bows (page 35)
shell border (page 22)
tube No. 5

1. Position the cake on the cake board so that the cake is slightly to the front.

2. Roll out pale egg-yellow plastic icing, large enough to cover the cake and the board.

3. Smooth the icing over the cake, then lift the icing at intervals and support it with cotton wool to create the hat brim.

4. Using pale apricot modelling paste, mould nine roses, following the instructions on page 39.

5. Mould several hyacinths from white modelling paste, following the instructions on page 40.

6. Form the roses, hyacinths and ribbon bows into sprays and position them around the front half of the brim as shown, attaching them with royal icing.

7. Pipe a shell border around the edge of the brim with white royal icing in a No. 5 star tube.

Posy in a Parasol

This delightful cake is suitable for celebrating any special occasion.

INGREDIENTS

1 x 200 mm round cake (page 12)
1 kg pale green plastic icing (page 14)
green and white royal icing (page 14)
pink, lemon-yellow, white, blue and green modelling paste (page 14)

MATERIALS AND DECORATIONS

1 x 250 mm round cake board
shell border (page 22)
tubes Nos. 0, 1, 5
pink and pale lemon roses (page 39)
5-petal flower cutters (2 sizes)
ball tool
tiny white and blue daisies (page 43)
daisy cutter
pattern for leaves (page 158), parasol and dove's wing (page 162)
pin
anger tool

1. Cover the cake and board with pale green plastic icing and pipe a small shell border around the edge of the cake board with green royal icing in a No. 5 star tube.

2. Mould nine tiny roses from pink modelling paste and nine from pale lemon modelling paste, following the instructions on page 39 Steps 1, 2, 9 and 10.

3. Shape the petals, carefully overlapping them slightly, and curving out the outer edge of each petal.

4. Cut out five-petal rounded blossoms from pink and pale lemon modelling paste using the larger flower cutter. Flute the edges and hollow each petal slightly with a ball tool. Wet the centre and attach

one to each half rose. Curve out the outer edge of each petal.

5. Roll out white and blue modelling paste and cut out a number of tiny star-shaped daisies with a daisy cutter. Hollow the flowers slightly. Pipe a small dot of green royal icing into each centre and allow them to dry.

6. Cut out a number of leaves from green modelling paste and vein them with a pin. Allow them to dry.

7. Hand mould the dove from white modelling paste, following the steps in the photograph.

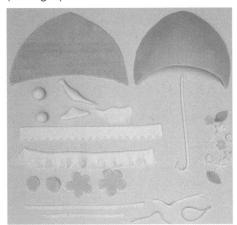

8. Roll out pink modelling paste and cut out the parasol and shape it over a mould or suitable shape to dry.

9. Cut a narrow strip from white modelling paste, scalloped along one edge and long enough to fit the bottom of the parasol. Frill the edges with an anger tool and attach it to the parasol with royal icing.

10. Roll a long piece of white modelling paste to form the handle and attach the parasol and handle to the cake with royal icing.

11. Tuck a small piece of plastic icing inside the parasol.

12. Pipe fine dots or shells around the parasol and decorate the parasol with the tiny design as shown using white royal icing in a No. 0 writing tube.

13. Decorate the top edge of the cake with stems and leaves with green royal icing in a No. 0 writing tube.

14. Roll out pink and lemon-yellow modelling paste and cut out flowers with the smaller flower cutter. Hollow the flowers slightly with a ball tool and pipe a dot of green royal icing into their centres. Attach the flowers to the top edge with royal icing to complete the design.

15. Insert the stems of the roses and daisies into the plastic icing under the parasol to make a full arrangement. Add some leaves, attaching them with a little royal icing.

16. Cut 2 mm wide ribbon from white modelling paste, cut a V-shape into the ends and make a number of loops for the ribbon bows. Attach them to the top of the parasol and to the handle.

17. Attach the dove to the top of the cake with royal icing.

18. Attach a rose to the top of the parasol and daisies and moulded flowers to the bow on the handle.

19. Attach the roses and leaves around the base of the cake with royal icing.

Fruit Basket

These hand-moulded miniature fruit are an unusual decoration, making this cake suitable for many occasions.

INGREDIENTS

1 x 250 mm round cake (page 12)
vegetable fat
brown pastillage (page 15)
brown and cream royal icing (page 14)
marzipan (page 15) and white plastic
   icing
gum Arabic glaze (page 15)
1 kg cream plastic icing (page 14)

MATERIALS AND DECORATIONS

1 x 300 mm round cake board
small glass bowl
basket weave (page 28)
tubes Nos. 1, 7, 98 (Ateco)
roping (page 28)
pattern sizes for fruit (page 161)
leaf-green, lemon-yellow, red, egg-
   yellow, orange, green, brown and
   purple food colouring
knife
ribbon inserter
pair of scissors
whole cloves
brown, green, rose-pink, orange and red
   brush-on powder
fine paintbrush
grater
pull-up and pull-away shell borders
   (page 22)
loops, scallops and dots (page 21)

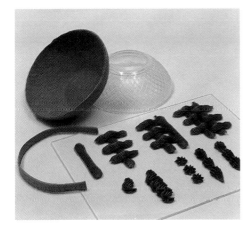

1. Rub vegetable fat onto the outside of a small glass bowl. Roll out brown pastillage and shape it over the bowl, cutting away the excess. Remove the pastillage and allow it to dry. Pipe a basket weave pattern over the bowl with brown royal icing in a No. 98 Ateco tube.

2. Roll out brown pastillage and cut a strip, long enough to fit the top of the basket, for the handle. Curve the strip and allow it to dry. Pipe roping onto the handle with brown royal icing in a No. 7 star tube.

3. When the basket and handle are dry, attach the handle to the basket with royal icing.

4. Mix together well equal quantities of plastic icing and marzipan and divide the moulding paste into smaller pieces.

5. Using the patterns on page 161 as a guide to the size of each fruit, make the fruit as follows:

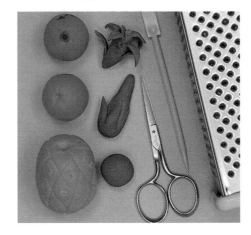

Pineapple: Mould light orange moulding paste to form a pineapple, marking it with a knife and a sharp-pointed tool (such as a ribbon inserter). Roll green moulding paste into a ball and cut the leaves, as shown, with a pair of scissors. Attach the leaves to the top of the pineapple with royal icing.

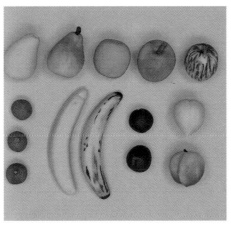

Granny Smith apple: Add leaf-green and lemon-yellow food colouring to a piece of moulding paste and shape it as shown. Push a whole clove into the base of the apple and attach a small 'stalk' of brown moulding paste to the top. When the apple is dry, dust it with brown and green brush-on powder.

Starking apple: Mould very light lemon-yellow paste to form an apple and when dry, streak with red food colouring on a fine brush.

Orange: Add orange food colouring with a touch of egg-yellow to a piece of moulding paste and shape it to form an orange. Roll the orange against a grater to create the rough effect on the skin. Attach a small rough star-shaped piece of green paste to the top of the orange. When dry, dust the orange with a little green and orange brush-on powder.

Pear: Add lemon-yellow food colouring with a touch of leaf-green to a piece of moulding paste and mould into a pear shape. Push a whole clove into the base of the pear and add a brown moulding paste 'stalk' to the top. When the pear is dry, brush it lightly with rose-pink brush-on powder.

Banana: Colour moulding paste with lemon-yellow and add a touch of egg-yellow food colouring. Roll the paste into a ball and then into a 'sausage-shape', moulding the paste to obtain the rounded, flattened banana shape. When dry, dust the banana with green and brown brush-on powder. Paint the details with various shades of brown and a fine paintbrush.

Peach: Colour moulding paste lemon-yellow and shape it into a peach. Attach a small brown 'stalk' of moulding paste. When dry, brush the peach with red brush-on powder.

Plum: Add purple food colouring to a small piece of moulding paste and shape it into a plum. When dry, glaze the plum with water or gum Arabic glaze.

6. Cover the cake with cream plastic icing. Pipe a border of pull-up shells around the base and pull-away shells around the top edge of the cake with cream royal icing in a No. 7 star tube.

7. Pipe loops around the base and scallops and dots around the top edge with brown royal icing in a No. 1 writing tube.

8. Attach the basket to the top of the cake with a little royal icing and fill the basket with fruit. Arrange more fruit around the basket as shown, attaching them to the cake with royal icing.

NOTE: To create realistic fruit, use real fruit as a guide, always beginning with the largest fruits first to ensure the correct proportions.

Going Gardening

INGREDIENTS
1 x 250 mm round cake (page 12)
1 kg apricot plastic icing (page 14)
apricot royal icing (page 14)
green, yellow, pale pink and yellow
   modelling paste (page 14)
pale brown pastillage (page 15)

MATERIALS AND DECORATIONS
1 x 300 mm round cake board
greaseproof paper
half-round crimper
tubes Nos. 0, 1, 42
shell border
scalloped cutter
anger tool
tiny flower cutter
egg white
non-toxic silver powder
little vodka, gin or caramel oil flavouring
patterns for wheelbarrow (page 165),
   leaves (page 158)
primroses (page 64)
daffodils (page 64)
blossoms (page 76)
hyacinths (page 40)
daisy cutter
pin
covered florist wire
leaf cutter

1. Cut two strips of greaseproof paper approximately 25 mm wide and long enough to go around the cake.

2. Cover the cake with apricot plastic icing and position the strips of greaseproof paper around the cake. Place one strip in line with the base of the cake and the second in line with the top edge.

3. Crimp two lines around the side of the cake with a half-round crimper using the greaseproof strips to guide you.

4. Embroider tiny flowers, in assorted pastel shades, and leaves between the two lines of crimping with a No. 0 or 1 writing tube. Trim the crimping with royal icing in a No. 1 writing tube.

5. Pipe shells along the base of the cake with apricot royal icing in a No. 42 star tube.

6. For the hat, use a ball of modelling paste the colour of your choice and roll out some of the paste all around to form the brim. Cut the outer edge with a scalloped cutter and frill it with an anger tool.

7. Cut a thin strip of modelling paste to form a ribbon and attach it to the dry hat. Cut out tiny flowers in assorted colours with a flower cutter and attach them to the ribbon with a little egg white.

8. Roll out a piece of green modelling paste quite thickly and cut out the gloves.

9. Shape the tools from modelling paste, then paint them with silver powder mixed with a little alcohol or caramel oil.

10. Cut out the parts of the wheelbarrow from pale brown pastillage, remembering to turn over the pieces occasionally to allow them to dry thoroughly. Assemble the wheelbarrow with royal icing.

11. Make primroses and daffodils according to the instructions on page 64, Steps 5-10.

12. Make blossoms from yellow modelling paste according to the instructions on page 76, Steps 4-7.

13. Make pale pink hyacinths according to the instructions on page 40.

14. To make the daisies, roll out white modelling paste and cut out the flowers with a small daisy cutter. Mark the petals with a pin. Bend over the end of a piece of covered wire and then bend the hook over sideways. Thread the straight end of the wire through the centre of the daisy.

15. Roll a small piece of yellow modelling paste into a ball and press it against a piece of net to mark it. Attach it to the centre of the flower with a little egg white. Allow the flower to dry.

16. Using green modelling paste, cut out a few leaves with a leaf cutter or with a pattern (page 158) and a sharp knife. Attach the leaves to florist wire and allow them to dry in a natural shape.

17. Place a piece of modelling paste inside the wheelbarrow and arrange the flowers and leaves so that the wheelbarrow is filled.

18. Position the wheelbarrow, hat, tools and gloves on top of the cake and attach them with a little royal icing.

This cake, topped with its flower-filled wheelbarrow, will delight the enthusiastic gardener.

White Christmas

The red loops, piped when the cake is upside down, add colour to this unusual and elegant Christmas cake.

INGREDIENTS

1 x 200 mm hexagonal cake (page 12)
750 g white plastic icing (page 14)
white and red royal icing (page 14)
white and red modelling paste (page 14)

MATERIALS AND DECORATIONS

1 x 250 mm hexagonal cake board
star border (page 22)
tubes Nos. 0, 1, 2, 4, 7
patterns for embroidery (page 160), holly
    leaves (page 158)
flat paintbrush No. 0
cotton wool
canister
small and medium blossom cutters
black stamens
non-toxic gold powder
gin, vodka or caramel oil flavouring
fine paintbrush

1. Cover the cake with white plastic icing and *allow it to dry.*

2. Pipe a star border all around the base of the cake on the board with white royal icing in a No. 7 star tube. Allow it to dry.

3. On the top of the cake, mark the centre of each of the six sides and trace the embroidery design onto the cake.

4. Pipe the stems with white royal icing in a No. 0 writing tube.

5. Add a small quantity of water to white royal icing, put it into a No. 2 writing tube and, working on one petal or leaf at a time, pipe around the leaves and around the rounded part of each petal. With a No. 0 flat tole paintbrush, brush the icing from the outer edge towards the centre of the leaf or flower, leaving a thickish edge around each shape (see page 24).

6. Pipe small white dots in the centre of each flower and tiny red dots near the flowers with No. 0 writing tubes.

7. Place a piece of cotton wool, approximately 100 mm in diameter on top of a canister. Very carefully turn the cake over so that it is upside down and resting on the cotton wool on the canister.

8. Fill a No. 1 writing tube with red royal icing and pipe three loops of different lengths from the first star to the third star. Pipe the next three loops from the second star to the fourth star, and so on. After completing a few sets of loops, it is preferable to allow the icing to set before continuing. Leave the cake on the canister until the loops are completely dry and then carefully turn the cake over.

9. Should you feel less confident about completing the embroidery before turning the cake over to execute the loops, pipe the loops first. Once they are thoroughly dry, turn the cake over and do Steps 4, 5 and 6.

10. Roll out white modelling paste and cut out holly leaves and blossoms in different sizes.

11. Roll red modelling paste into small balls to form the holly berries. Add a black stamen to each berry.

12. Mix the gold powder with a little gin, vodka or caramel oil flavouring and paint the edges of the holly leaves.

13. Attach the flowers, leaves and berries to the centre of the cake, and berries and leaves to each corner with royal icing.

Merry Christmas

Holly and ribbons give this cake a delightful, festive note.

INGREDIENTS
1 x 200 x 150 mm rectangular cake
(page 12)
1 kg white plastic icing (page 14)
green, white and red modelling paste
(page 14)
red, green and white royal icing (page 14)

MATERIALS AND DECORATIONS
1 x 250 x 200 mm rectangular cake board
straight-edge cutter
egg white
cotton wool
tubes Nos. 1, 3, 5
holly leaf cutter
pin
shell border (page 22)

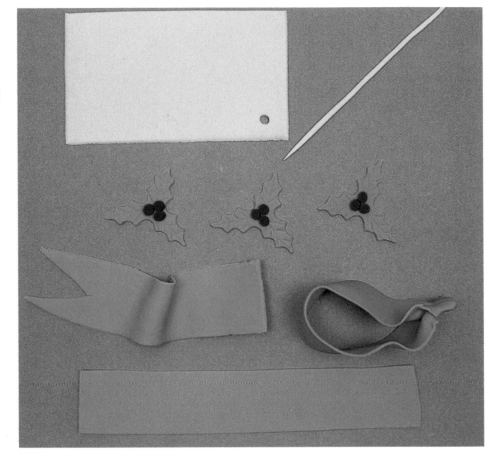

1. Cover the cake with white plastic icing.

2. Roll out green modelling paste and cut 15 mm wide lengths of ribbon with a straight-edge cutter.

3. With egg white or water, attach a length of this ribbon across the cake from the board on one side to the board on the other.

4. Cut about eight 60 x 15 mm lengths of green modelling paste and loop them to form a bow. Use cotton wool or sponge to support the loops until they are set.

5. Cut two 50 x 15 mm lengths of green paste and cut a 'V' out of each end. Shape the paste to look like ribbon.

6. Attach the ribbons and ribbon loops to the cake with soft royal icing.

7. Cut a 60 x 40 mm rectangle of white modelling paste for a tag and cut a hole out of the corner with a No. 3 writing tube.

8. Roll a small piece of white modelling paste to form the string and thread it through the hole in the tag.

9. Pipe a message onto the tag with red royal icing in a No. 1 writing tube and edge the tag with little dots.

10. Cut 3-in-1 holly leaves from green modelling paste and vein them with a pin.

11. Roll red modelling paste into small red berries, press a small hollow into each with a sharp pointed object and attach three to each leaf with egg white.

12. Position the leaves and berries on the cake so that they resemble designs on wrapping paper and attach them with royal icing.

13. Attach the tag to the cake with the string under the bow.

14. Pipe a shell border around the base of the cake with green royal icing in a No. 5 star tube.

Stained Glass Window

Piping jelly is used to create a three-dimensional effect on this unusual Christmas cake. Trace the design directly onto the cake or use the Wafer Painting technique described on page 49.

INGREDIENTS
1 x 200 mm oval cake (page 12)
1 kg white plastic icing (page 14)
grey royal icing (page 14)

MATERIALS AND DECORATIONS
1 x 250 mm oval cake board
pattern for picture (page 172)
tracing paper
pencil
food colouring in various shades
piping jelly in various shades
paintbrushes Nos. 00000, 1, 2
tubes Nos. 1, 42
shell border (page 22)

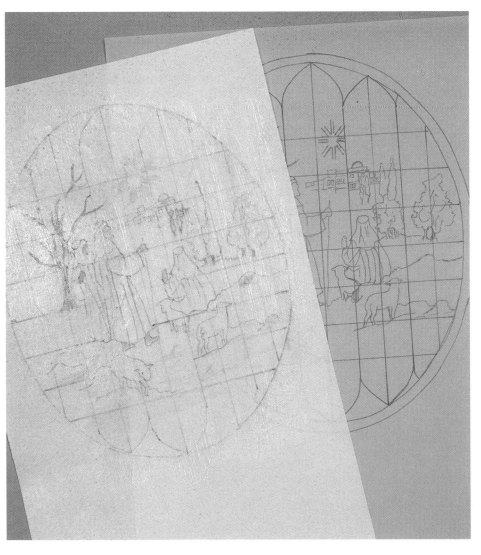

1. Cover the cake and the cake board with white plastic icing.

2. Trace the picture onto a piece of tracing paper and go over the back of the design with a soft pencil. Transfer the picture to the top of the cake by rubbing gently over the design with a pencil. If you are using the Wafer Painting technique, use a non-toxic felt-tipped pen to trace the design onto the smooth side of the rice paper. Cut out the oval shape and brush clear or neutral piping jelly over the entire surface of the design with a firm, flat brush. Allow it to dry thoroughly.

3. Using food colouring and very little water on your brush, paint the background details.

4. If you are using the Wafer Painting technique, turn the picture over and paint the surface with clear or neutral piping jelly. Position the picture on top of the cake, touching it down in places with the back of a paintbrush.

5. Following the instructions on page 46, pipe piping jelly onto the clothes of the figures to create a 3-D effect.

6. Pipe the lines of the window onto the picture with grey royal icing in a No. 1 writing tube. Do not take the lines through the figures.

7. Pipe a shell border around the top edge of the cake and around the edge of the board with grey royal icing in a No. 42 star tube.

Strawberry Celebration

This colourful cake with a fruity theme can be adapted to suit any occasion.

INGREDIENTS
1 x 250 mm octagonal cake (page 12)
1,5 kg white plastic icing (page 14)
yellow royal icing (page 14)
red, green and white modelling paste
    (page 14)

MATERIALS AND DECORATIONS
1 x 300 mm octagonal cake board
pattern for lettering (page 174), leaves
    (page 159)
tracing paper
tube No. 1
non-toxic gold powder
little gin, vodka or caramel oil flavouring
toothpick
florist wire
small star-shaped cutter
egg white
5-petal flower cutter
yellow stamens
pin

1. Cover the cake and the board with white plastic icing.

2. Using the lettering on page 174, trace 'Happy Birthday' onto a piece of tracing paper and transfer it to the top of the cake by going over the letters with a sharp object. Outline the letters with yellow royal icing in a No. 1 writing tube and then flood them with yellow royal icing, following the instructions for Floodwork on page 31. Mix the gold powder with a little gin, vodka or caramel oil flavouring and paint the letters once they have dried.

3. Mould red modelling paste into strawberries of different sizes, including some tiny 'young' ones with the calyx still wrapped around the fruit.

4. Prick tiny holes all over the strawberries with a toothpick. Pipe a dot of yellow royal icing into each hole using a No. 1 writing tube. Smooth off each dot with your fingers. Insert a piece of florist wire into each strawberry and bud.

5. Cut small stars out of green modelling paste for the hulls and attach them to the strawberries with egg white.

6. Roll out white modelling paste and cut out the flowers using a flower cutter. Hollow them slightly and thread a piece of florist wire that has been bent at one end through the centre of each flower.

7. Pipe yellow royal icing into each flower to form the centre and insert a few small, yellow stamens into the icing while it is still wet. Allow to dry thoroughly.

8. Roll out green modelling paste and cut out leaves using the pattern on page 159. Vein the leaves with a pin as shown.

9. Attach the strawberries, leaves and flowers to the cake with royal icing.

Lady in the Garden

This attractive design is created by using the Wafer Painting technique. Moulded forget-me-nots are made separately and attached to the cake with royal icing. Piped leaves are added between the flowers.

NOTE: Before attempting this design, please read the instructions for the *Wafer Painting technique* on page 49.

INGREDIENTS

1 x 200 mm round cake (page 12)
1,5 kg pale blue plastic icing (page 14)
white and green royal icing (page 14)
modelling paste in assorted pastel shades (page 14)

MATERIALS AND DECORATIONS

1 x 250 mm round cake board
shell border (page 22)
tubes Nos. 1, 3, 42, leaf tube
snail's trail (page 21)
rice paper
patterns for picture (page 165), lettering (page 174)
fine paintbrush
brown non-toxic fibre-tip pen
clear piping jelly
pink, blue, brown and copper or flesh-coloured food colouring
paper towel
waxed paper
forget-me-nots (page 40)
non-toxic gold powder
little gin, vodka or caramel oil flavouring

1. Cover the cake and board with the pale blue plastic icing.

2. Pipe a small shell border around the edge of the board with a No. 42 star tube and a snail's trail around the base of the cake with a No. 1 writing tube.

3. Following the instructions for Wafer Painting on page 49, cut a 165 mm diameter circle of rice paper and trace the picture onto the smooth side with the fibre-tip pen. Using the lettering on page 174, trace 'Happy Birthday' onto the rice paper at the top of the picture.

4. Paint clear piping jelly very thinly and evenly over the smooth side of the rice paper.

5. Paint the picture, remembering to use as little water as possible on your brush. Keep a piece of paper towel handy to wipe off the excess water.

6. Allow the picture to dry, turn it over onto a piece of waxed paper and paint the back with clear or neutral piping jelly, or alternatively, paint a circle of piping jelly onto the top of the cake. Position the picture on the cake.

7. Mould forget-me-nots from modelling paste in assorted colours and attach them to the cake with royal icing. Pipe the leaves with green royal icing in a leaf tube or a small cone cut accordingly.

8. Use royal icing in a No. 1 writing tube to pipe over the lettering. Allow it to dry. Mix the gold powder with a little alcohol or caramel oil and paint the lettering.

9. Pipe a border of small shells with a No. 42 star tube, or beading with a No. 3 writing tube, around the edge of the rice paper circle.

Windsurfer

The orchids add a touch of femininity to this cake for a young windsurfer who is coming of age.

INGREDIENTS
1 x 250 mm square cake (page 12)
1 kg pale apricot plastic icing (page 14)
white, red, yellow, black and
　flesh-coloured royal icing (page 14)
apricot and green modelling paste
　(page 14)

MATERIALS AND DECORATIONS
1 x 300 mm square cake board
pattern for windsurfer (page 169),
　numerals and lettering (page 175),
　leaves (page 158)
tracing paper
blue and green brush-on powders
tubes Nos. 1, 7
small paintbrush
shell border (page 22)
cymbidium orchids (page 45)
leaf cutter
pin

1. Cover the cake with pale apricot plastic icing.

2. Trace the picture, lettering and numerals onto tracing paper and transfer the designs to the cake by going over them with a sharp object.

3. Mark the horizon line and shade the 'sea' with the blue and green brush-on powders.

4. Outline the picture, lettering and numerals with royal icing in a No. 1 writing tube and flood the picture directly on the cake, following the instructions for Floodwork on page 31.

5. Pipe a little white royal icing on the waves to form foam and rough it up a little with a small paintbrush.

6. Pipe a shell border around the base and top edge of the cake with white royal icing in a No. 7 star tube.

7. Make two medium-sized cymbidium orchids in apricot modelling paste by following the instructions on page 45. Cut out some leaves in green modelling paste with either a leaf cutter or with a pattern and a sharp knife, and vein them with a pin or leaf veiner. Attach an orchid with a few leaves on opposite corners and a few leaves to the base of the cake as shown.

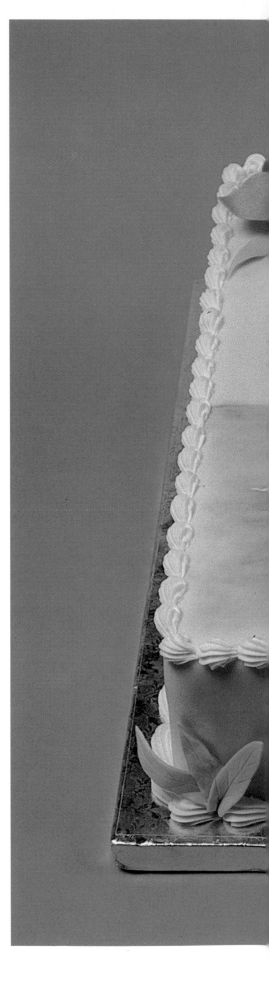

Coming of Age

The choice of decorations on this cake is endless and can be varied to fit the activities of the recipient.

INGREDIENTS
1 x 250 mm oval cake (page 12)
1 kg white plastic icing (page 14)
white, blue, light brown, black and red modelling paste (page 14)
pale blue and white royal icing (page 14)
white pastillage (page 15)

MATERIALS AND DECORATIONS
1 x 300 mm oval cake board
blue brush-on powder
shell border (page 22)
scrolls (page 22)
tubes Nos. 0, 1, 7, 42
food colouring
fine paintbrush
domed flower nail
red rosebuds (page 39)
pattern for plaques (page 166), lettering and numerals (page 175)
cotton wool

1. Cover the cake with white plastic icing and brush around the base of the cake with blue brush-on powder.

2. Pipe a shell border around the base and scrolls on the top edge of the cake with blue royal icing in a No. 7 star tube.

3. Mould the baby's bottle and bib from white modelling paste and the bootees from blue paste according to the photographs. Pipe a tiny design on the bootees in white and on the bib in pale blue royal icing.

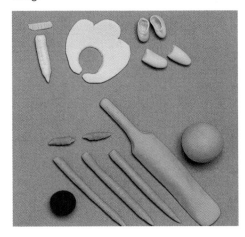

4. Roll out pieces of white and blue modelling paste and cut out the school book, making a cover and pages as shown. When dry, paint the details onto the open pages.

5. Mould the cricket bat, wickets and bails from light brown modelling paste and allow them to dry.

6. For the mortar board, roll out black modelling paste and cut out a square and a circle, shaping the circle over a dome-shaped flower nail to form the crown. Roll out red modelling paste and cut out the tassle as shown. Assemble the mortar board with royal icing.

7. Roll up a thin rectangle of white modelling paste to form a scroll and place a ribbon made from red modelling paste around it.

8. Make two rosebuds according to the instructions on page 39. Cut out a small square of white modelling paste, pipe on the lettering with blue royal icing in a No. 0 or 1 writing tube and attach it to the rosebud with a strip of white modelling paste.

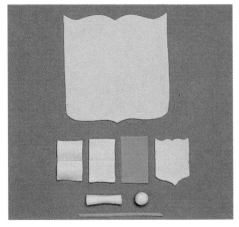

9. Roll out a piece of white pastillage or modelling paste and cut a large plaque for the top of the cake using the pattern on page 166 as a guide. Allow the plaque to dry thoroughly.

10. Transfer the name and '21 today' onto the plaque by tracing over the lettering and numerals with a sharp object. Outline the design with blue royal icing in a No. 0 writing tube and then flood the name and '21 today' with blue royal icing, following the instructions for Floodwork on page 31. Trim the design with white royal icing in a No. 0 writing tube, if desired.

11. Trim the edge of the plaque with blue royal icing in a No. 42 star tube. Attach the plaque to the cake with royal icing, supporting it with cotton wool until the icing has set.

12. Cut out eight small plaques in white modelling paste according to the pattern on page 166. Pipe '21' on each with blue royal icing in a No. 1 writing tube and attach them to the sides of the cake with a little royal icing.

13. Arrange the items on top of the cake, attaching them with royal icing.

Sweet Sixteen

A romantic cake for that special young lady who is turning sixteen.

INGREDIENTS
1 x 200 mm heart-shaped cake (page 12)
1 x 250 mm square cake
2 kg pale pink plastic icing (page 14)
white and pink royal icing (page 14)
white and pink modelling paste (page 14)

MATERIALS AND DECORATIONS
sloping pillar stand
1 x 200 mm heart-shaped cake board
1 x 300 mm square cake board
patterns for numerals (page 175),
    scalloped ovals and hearts
    (page 162)
tubes Nos. 0, 1, 2, 42, 43
shell border (page 22)
snail's trail (page 21)
carnations (page 41)
pink brush-on powder
cornflour
frill ruler
straight-edge cutter
steel-lined knitting needle
silver ribbon bows
pin

1. The sloping pillar stand, used to support the top tier, comes with spikes which prevent the cake board from slipping off the stand. First drill four holes into the base of the heart-shaped cake board to match the positions of the spikes on the stand.

2. Cover the heart-shaped cake with pale pink plastic icing, taking the icing over the edges of the cake board.

3. Cover the square cake with pale pink plastic icing.

4. Trace the numerals onto the centre of the heart-shaped cake and outline them with white royal icing in a No. 1 writing tube.

5. Flood the numerals with white royal icing, following the instructions for Floodwork on page 31, and allow them to dry.

6. Cut out four scalloped ovals from white modelling paste and four hearts from pink modelling paste and attach them to the sides of the square cake with royal icing.

7. Pipe a shell border around the base of each cake with a No. 43 star tube.

8. Pipe a snail's trail around the numerals and the scalloped ovals with pink royal icing in a No. 0 writing tube. With the same tube, pipe tiny flowers and leaves onto the numerals.

9. Make several small white carnations, following the instructions on page 41, and set them aside to dry.

10. Add cornflour to pink brush-on powder to create a pale pink and brush the edges of the carnations with the powder.

11. For the frill around the heart-shaped cake, cut out two strips, each with one edge scalloped and the other straight, from white modelling paste. Frill the scalloped edge with a steel-lined knitting needle, leaving a plain border along the straight edge.

12. Pipe a line of royal icing along the straight edge of one frill and attach it to the cake. Repeat the procedure with the other half of the frill. Prop up the frill, if necessary, until it is dry.

13. Pipe a snail's trail along the edge of the frill with pink royal icing in a No. 2 writing tube.

14. Form a crescent-shaped spray with the carnations and two silver ribbon bows and attach the spray to the top of the heart-shaped cake with royal icing.

15. Make up three more sprays with carnations and ribbon bows and attach them to the top of the bottom tier.

16. Trace around the circle of the sloping stand with a pin and pipe a shell border around it with a No. 42 star tube and white royal icing.

17. Replace the stand and position the heart-shaped cake on it.

On the Grapevine

This attractive cake is suitable for a man or a woman and can be adapted to celebrate any occasion.

INGREDIENTS

1 x 275 mm hexagonal cake (page 12)
white, purple and pale green royal icing (page 14)
1,5 kg pale green plastic icing (page 14)
purple and green modelling paste (page 14)
gum Arabic glaze (page 15)

MATERIALS AND EQUIPMENT

1 x 325 mm hexagonal cake board
pattern for floodwork lettering (page 174), grape leaves (page 159)
pencil
tracing paper
piece of glass
tubes Nos. 1, 42
shell border (page 22)
light green florist tape
fuse wire
large pin
anger tool

1. Using the lettering on page 174, trace 'Happy Birthday' onto tracing paper. Turn the paper over and go over the lettering with a soft pencil. Place the paper under a piece of glass so that the lettering reads back-to-front. Outline the letters with royal icing in a No. 1 writing tube to make a glass stencil. Allow the icing to dry thoroughly.

2. Cover the cake and the cake board with pale green plastic icing and immediately press the glass stencil onto the centre of the cake.

3. Outline the letters with purple royal icing in a No. 1 writing tube and then flood the letters with the same shade, following the instructions for Floodwork on page 31. Allow the lettering to dry thoroughly.

4. Pipe a shell border around the top edge and around the base of the cake using a No. 42 star tube.

5. Cut light green florist tape into four and tape short lengths of fuse wire.

6. Roll purple modelling paste into small balls to form the grapes and attach them to the covered fuse wire.

7. Roll out green modelling paste and cut out the grape leaves in a variety of sizes.

8. Vein the leaves with a pin as shown and flute the edges with an anger tool.

9. When dry, paint the grapes and leaves with gum Arabic glaze.

10. Form the grapes into bunches and attach them and the leaves to the cake.

Bathing Beauty

A touch of fun for a gentleman who has a special occasion to celebrate.

INGREDIENTS

1 x 150 x 200 mm cake (page 12)
500 g white plastic icing (page 14)
red modelling paste (page 14)
flesh-coloured, red, yellow, and white
   royal icing (page 14)

MATERIALS AND DECORATIONS

1 x 180 x 230 mm cake board
pattern for pin-up (page 168)
fine paintbrush
small brush
red and brown food colouring
shell border (page 22)
tubes Nos. 1, 6, 7

1. Cover the cake with white plastic icing and trace the picture of the girl onto the top of the cake by going over the design with a sharp object.

2. Roll out red modelling paste and cut out six large and six small hearts.

3. Outline the girl's body with flesh-coloured royal icing and the bikini with red. Flood the girl's body, then the bikini, following the instructions for Floodwork on page 31.

4. Outline and flood the hair using slightly stiffer yellow royal icing so that it can be brushed into shape.

5. Paint on the features with brown and red food colouring on a fine paintbrush.

6. Paint on the shoes with red food colouring and a fine paintbrush.

7. Attach the hearts to the top of the cake with water, egg white or royal icing. Paint red lines from the hearts to the pin-up with red food colouring on a fine paintbrush.

8. Pipe a shell border around the top edge of the cake with red royal icing in a No. 6 star tube.

9. Pipe a shell border around the base of the cake with white royal icing in a No. 7 star tube.

10. Add small red dots above the white shell border and on the inside of the red shell border using a No. 1 writing tube.

Ballet Trio

Floodwork, tube work and moulding techniques combine to decorate this delightful birthday cake.

INGREDIENTS
1 x 250 mm trefoil cake (or three small round cakes cut and joined) (page 12)
1 kg cream plastic icing (page 14)
orange, flesh-coloured or coppertone, brown and yellow royal icing (page 14)
pale apricot, orange, cream and green modelling paste (page 14)

MATERIALS AND DECORATIONS
1 x 300 mm round cake board
shell border (page 22)
tubes Nos. 1, 42, 43, 101 (Ateco)
tracing paper
patterns for ballet dancers (page 163), leaves (page 158)
orange, brown and rose-pink food colouring
fine paintbrush
straight-edge cutter
medium and small flower cutter
ball tool
pin

1. Cover the cake with cream plastic icing and pipe a shell border around the base of the cake with orange royal icing in a No. 42 star tube.

2. Make a tracing of the ballet dancer and transfer the design onto each scallop on the top of the cake by going over the design with a sharp object.

3. Outline the faces, arms, legs and feet with flesh-coloured or coppertone royal icing in a No. 1 writing tube.

4. Outline the dresses in orange royal icing in a No. 1 writing tube.

5. Flood the faces, arms, legs and feet of each dancer with flesh-coloured or coppertone royal icing, following the instructions for Floodwork on page 31. Allow the dancers to dry.

6. Pipe small frills onto the skirts and bodices with orange icing in a No. 101 Ateco tube, starting with the lowest frill.

7. When dry, paint on the ballet shoes using orange food colouring and very little water on a fine paintbrush. Paint the eyes with brown and the lips with rose-pink food colouring.

8. Pipe a little soft brown royal icing onto each dancer's head to form hair.

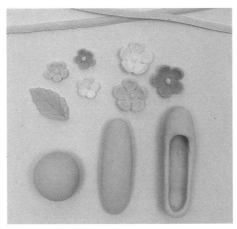

9. Hand mould six little ballet shoes from pale apricot modelling paste and attach them to the cake with royal icing.

10. Roll out pale apricot modelling paste and cut out twelve 2 mm wide ribbons with a straight-edge cutter and attach two to each shoe with a little water or royal icing.

11. Roll out orange, pale apricot and cream modelling paste and cut out medium and small flowers with the flower cutters. Hollow the flowers slightly with a small ball tool and pipe a small dot of yellow royal icing into the centre of each flower.

12. Roll out green modelling paste and cut out several leaves, veining them with a pin. Attach the flowers and the leaves to the cake with royal icing.

On Target

A cake with a masculine theme that will appeal to the sportsman in your family.

INGREDIENTS
1 x 250 mm hexagonal cake (page 12)
1 kg white plastic icing (page 14)
yellow, black, green and red royal icing (page 14)
green and white modelling paste (page 14)

MATERIALS AND DECORATIONS
1 x 300 mm hexagonal cake board
patterns for dartboard (page 173),
   lettering (page 174), flights (page 173)
tubes Nos. 0 or 1, 7
cocktail sticks
non-toxic gold powder
gin, vodka or caramel oil flavouring
paintbrush
shell border (page 22)

1. Cover the cake with white plastic icing.

2. Trace the dartboard, 'On target for a great day' and the name onto the top of the cake, or onto waxed paper if you wish to flood them separately.

3. Outline the lettering with yellow royal icing in a No. 0 or 1 writing tube.

4. Outline the dartboard sections with black royal icing in a No. 1 writing tube.

5. Flood the black sections of the dartboard, following the instructions for Floodwork on page 31, and allow these to dry.

6. Flood the lettering with yellow royal icing.

7. Flood the area around the dartboard with green royal icing.

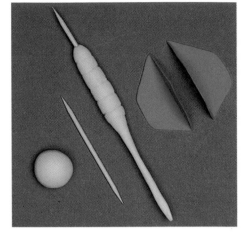

8. Make the darts by rolling out green modelling paste and cutting out two flights for each dart.

9. Fold each flight in half and leave it to dry thoroughly on the edge of a table or flower stand.

10. Roll a piece of white modelling paste into a 'sausage' and insert a cocktail stick that has been dampened with water into one end.

11. Roll the other end of the 'sausage' into a thin stem and press a groove lengthwise into each side of the stem to accommodate the flights. Allow the darts to dry.

12. Place a flight on a level surface and pipe some royal icing part way along its length. Attach the thin stem to this flight and then attach the second flight with royal icing. Set aside to dry thoroughly.

13. Mix the gold powder with a little vodka, gin or caramel oil flavouring and paint the darts and the cocktail sticks as shown.

14. Flood the yellow sections of the dartboard as well as the red dot in the centre.

15. Pipe a shell border along the top edges and around the base of the cake with yellow royal icing in a No. 7 star tube.

16. Attach the darts to the top of the cake with royal icing. If the lettering and dartboard have been flooded separately, attach them, together with the darts, to the top of the cake with royal icing.

Winning Streak

The Cocoa Painting technique is used to create this cake for horse lovers of any age.

INGREDIENTS

1 x 250 mm round cake (page 12)
1 kg pale blue plastic icing (page 14)
brown, dark and light blue modelling paste (page 14)
blue royal icing (page 14)

MATERIALS AND DECORATIONS

1 x 300 mm round cake board
pin
small plate
tracing paper
pattern for horse (page 170)
cocoa butter
cocoa powder
plastic artist's palette
toothpick
paintbrushes Nos. 00000, 0, 1, 2
hobby knife
plastic horseshoe mould
scalloped cutter
anger tool
shell border
tubes Nos. 42, 43
cotton wool

1. Cover the cake with pale blue plastic icing.

2. With a pin, draw a circle in the centre of the top of the cake using a small plate to guide you.

3. Make a tracing of the horse and transfer it to the circle by going over the design with a sharp object.

4. Place a small marble-size ball of cocoa butter into each of three hollows in an artist's palette and place the palette over a container of boiling water.

5. Add 5 mℓ cocoa powder to the first hollow, less to the second and even less to the third. Stir the cocoa powder into the cocoa butter with a toothpick. You will have three shades of brown.

6. Using a fine paintbrush, paint the horse's head, beginning with the lightest shade. Deepen the effect by using the medium and darkest shades. Do not paint over the whole area; leave highlighted areas to create a more realistic effect. If you wish, use a hobby knife to remove small areas of the cocoa mixture to create further highlights. (See Cocoa Painting on page 48.)

7. Press brown modelling paste into a plastic horseshoe mould and cut away the excess with a knife. Lift the paste out with a pin and allow the horseshoes to dry on a flat surface.

8. Roll out dark and pale blue modelling paste and cut out two scalloped circles from the dark blue and one from the pale blue paste.

9. Flute the edges of the circles with an anger tool.

10. Cut a 10 mm wide strip from each shade of blue and cut a 'V' out of one end of each strip to form the ribbons. Allow the ribbons to dry on a flat surface. Attach the circles to each other and allow them to set.

11. Pipe a small shell border around the centre circle and around the outer top edge of the cake with blue royal icing in a No. 42 star tube.

12. Pipe a shell border around the base of the cake with blue royal icing in a No. 43 star tube.

13. Attach the horseshoes to the cake with royal icing, supporting those on the top of the cake with cotton wool until the icing has dried.

14. Attach the ribbons and rosette to the top of the cake with royal icing.

Lone Ranger

Wafer Painting and Cocoa Painting combine successfully to create this delightful cake with a Western theme.

INGREDIENTS
1 x 200 mm round cake (page 12)
pale lemon-yellow plastic icing (page 14)
brown and green royal icing (page 14)

MATERIALS AND DECORATIONS
1 x 250 mm round cake board
rice paper
non-toxic fibre-tip pen
pattern for cowboy (page 171)
brown, red and yellow food colouring
fine paintbrush
clear or neutral piping jelly
tubes Nos. 2, 5 or 6, 7
shell border (page 22)
rope border (page 28)
cocoa powder
cocoa butter
curved shell border (page 22)

1. Cover the cake with pale lemon-yellow plastic icing.

2. Cut a 165 mm diameter circle of rice paper and trace the cowboy's head onto the smooth side with a brown non-toxic fibre-tip pen.

3. Following the instructions for Wafer Painting on page 49, complete the cowboy and then attach the picture to the cake with clear or neutral piping jelly.

4. Pipe a line around the edge of the cake board with brown royal icing, then flood the board with brown royal icing, following the instructions for Floodwork on page 31.

5. Pipe a small shell border around the edge of the rice paper circle with brown royal icing in a No. 2 writing tube.

6. Pipe a rope border around the top edge of the cake with brown royal icing in a No. 5 or 6 star tube.

7. Following the instructions for Cocoa Painting on page 48, paint the hills around the sides of the cake.

8. Figure pipe (page 35) cacti at intervals over the hills with green royal icing in a No. 7 star tube.

9. Once the floodwork on the board is dry, pipe a curved shell border along the edge with brown royal icing in a No. 7 star tube.

Grand Prix

A delightful cake for a Grand Prix racing fan.

INGREDIENTS

1 x 200 mm square cake (page 12)
750 g white plastic icing (page 14)
white and black modelling paste
   (page 14)
black, red and white royal icing (page 14)
neutral piping jelly

MATERIALS AND DECORATIONS

1 x 250 mm square cake board
patterns for racing car and flag
   (page 170)
black and red food colouring
paintbrush
cotton wool
tubes Nos. 1, 4 or 5

1. Cover the cake with white plastic icing.

2. Trace the picture of the car onto the cake.

3. Roll out white modelling paste and cut out a 100 x 60 mm rectangle for the large flag and two 25 x 35 mm rectangles for the small ones. Mark 20 mm squares on the large flag and 5 mm squares on the small flags. Paint alternate squares with black food colouring.

4. Shape the large flag as shown on page 170 by propping it up with cotton wool until it is dry.

5. Roll black modelling paste to form the poles for the flags and set them aside to dry.

6. Outline the parts of the car with black, red and white royal icing. Flood the body of the car with royal icing or piping jelly, following the instructions on pages 31 and 46 respectively.

7. Mix black royal icing with neutral piping jelly and flood the wheels slightly unevenly to give them a bit of texture.

8. Flood the remaining parts of the car and when they are dry, paint the numbers onto the front of the car with red food colouring.

9. Attach the large flag and pole to the top of the cake with royal icing.

10. Pipe large beads around the top and bottom edges of the cake with white royal icing in a No. 4 or 5 Ateco writing tube.

11. Using a No. 1 writing tube, add a dot of black royal icing to the beads around the base of the cake.

12. Attach the two small flags to the front of the cake.

Dancing Shoes

Hand-moulded ballet shoes and pink, white and blue blossoms will delight a young ballet fan.

INGREDIENTS

1 x 200 mm round cake (page 12)
750 g pale blue plastic icing (page 14)
pink, blue, white and green modelling
  paste (page 14)
pink and yellow royal icing (page 14)

MATERIALS AND DECORATIONS

1 x 250 mm round cake board
small, medium and large flower cutters
leaf cutter or pattern for leaves
  (page 158)
curved shell border (page 22)
tubes Nos. 2, 6
snail's trail (page 21)
straight-edge cutter

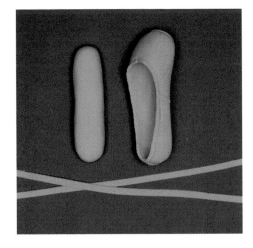 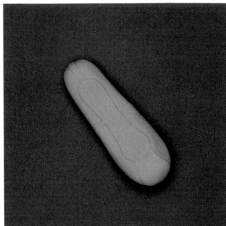

1. Cover the cake with pale blue plastic icing.

2. Hand mould a pair of ballet shoes from pink modelling paste.

3. Roll out pink, blue and white modelling paste and, following the instructions for forget-me-nots on page 40, cut out a number of blossoms using the three flower cutters.

4. Roll out green modelling paste and cut out a few leaves.

5. Pipe a curved shell border around the top edge of the cake with pink royal icing in a No. 6 star tube and a snail's trail around the base of the cake with a No. 2 writing tube.

6. Pipe a dot of yellow royal icing into the centre of each flower and attach a few small flowers and leaves to the side of the cake with royal icing.

7. Attach one ballet shoe to the cake with royal icing.

8. Roll out pink modelling paste and cut out four ribbons with a straight-edge cutter. Immediately attach a ribbon to each side of the shoe and allow them to drape over the sides of the cake.

9. Position the second shoe and attach the ribbons in the same way.

10. Attach a small blue flower to the front of each shoe with royal icing.

11. Attach the flowers and leaves to the top of the cake with royal icing.

12. With a straight-edge cutter, cut out a narrow strip, long enough to go around the cake, from pink modelling paste. Twist the strip and position it on top of the snail's trail as shown.

Clowning Around

This bright, happy clown will delight any child.

INGREDIENTS
1 x 200 mm round cake (page 12)
750 g white plastic icing (page 14)
red, green, yellow and flesh-coloured
   royal icing (page 14)

MATERIALS AND DECORATIONS
1 x 275 mm round cake board
pattern for clown and balloons
   (page 169)
tracing paper
soft pencil
red and brown food colouring
fine paintbrush
tubes Nos. 1, 7
shell border (page 22)

1. Cover the cake with white plastic icing.

2. Trace the clown and balloons onto the top of the cake using either the Glass Stencil method (page 28) or by going over the back of the design with a soft pencil, positioning it on the cake and softly tracing over the picture.

3. Following the instructions for Flood-work on page 31, outline the design in the relevant colours, then flood the clown in sections, remembering to allow each section to dry before flooding an adjacent section.

4. Paint on the eyes and mouth with food colouring on a fine paintbrush.

5. Pipe small yellow dots with a No. 1 writing tube to finish off the edge of the frill, hat and trousers.

6. Pipe the balloon strings with green royal icing in a No. 1 writing tube.

7. Support the cake at an angle and trace the balloons onto the sides of the cake. Outline the balloons with green and red royal icing, then flood each balloon, following the instructions on page 31. Pipe on the balloon strings with green royal icing in a No. 1 writing tube.

8. Trace 'Happy birthday' and the child's name onto the top of the cake and pipe over the letters with green royal icing in a No. 1 writing tube.

9. Pipe alternate green and red shells around the base of the cake with No. 7 star tubes.

My Alphabet

Floodwork has been used effectively to create this delightfully attractive birthday cake.

INGREDIENTS
1 x 230 x 320 mm cake (page 12)
2 kg white plastic icing (page 14)
white modelling paste (page 14)
yellow, grey, green and red royal icing
  (page 14)

MATERIALS AND DECORATIONS
1 x 250 x 400 mm cake board
knife
patterns for lettering (page 175), pictures
  (page 170)
tubes Nos. 1, 3, 5 or 6
shell border (page 22)

1. Cover the cake with the white plastic icing.

2. Mark the sides of the cake with a knife to resemble the pages of a book.

3. Knead together equal parts of white plastic icing and modelling paste, roll it out and cut out two 'pages' approximately 115 x 160 mm. Attach the pages to the top of the cake with water and turn back the corners as shown.

4. Transfer the letters and pictures to the top of the cake by going over the designs with a sharp object.

5. Outline the A, B, C, the first letter of the child's name, the numeral and the pictures with a No. 1 writing tube and royal icing in the relevant colours.

6. Flood the letters, numeral and pictures, following the instructions for Floodwork on page 31. When flooding the ball, remember to allow each section to dry before flooding the next.

7. Pipe on the rest of the name and 'today' with yellow royal icing in a No. 3 writing tube.

8. Pipe a shell border down the centre of the book and around the edge of the cake with yellow royal icing in a No. 5 or 6 star tube.

Swan Lake

*Fairies may be substituted for the dancers to create an
enchanted garden that would appeal to any young girl.*

INGREDIENTS

1 x 250 mm oval cake (page 12)
1,5 kg pale green plastic icing (page 14)
pale green, brown, white and yellow
    royal icing (page 14)
flesh-coloured, brown, white, pink,
    yellow, green and blue modelling paste
    (page 14)

MATERIALS AND DECORATIONS

1 x 300 mm oval cake board
shell border (page 22)
tubes Nos. 1, 2, 42, 233 (Ateco)
scissors
egg white
brown, red, black and yellow food
    colouring
fine paintbrush
small heart-shaped cutter
thin clear plastic
scalloped cutter
anger tool
blue piping jelly
blue bell-shaped flowers (page 40)
small daisy cutter
pin
covered florist wire
piece of net
forget-me-nots (page 40)
leaf cutter
candles
cocktail stick
pattern for fairy's wings (page 163)
rice paper
florist wire

1. Cover the cake and board with pale green plastic icing. Pipe a small shell border around the base of the cake and around the edge of the board with pale green royal icing in a No. 42 star tube.

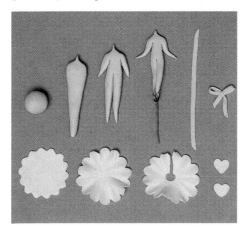

2. Make six little ballet dancers by rolling a ball of flesh-coloured modelling paste into a cylinder with one end narrower than the other. Pinch the paste in the centre of the wide end to form the neck.

3. Cut the arms and legs with a pair of scissors as shown. Roll each between thumb and forefinger to smooth. Set them aside to dry thoroughly.

4. Roll a small ball of modelling paste for the head and attach it immediately to the body with egg white or water.

5. Paint on the eyes and mouth using food colouring and a very fine paintbrush. Paint little ballet shoes onto each foot with red food colouring.

6. Allow the head to dry and then pipe on the hair with brown royal icing.

7. Roll out some white modelling paste and cut out 12 small hearts to form the bodice of each dancer's dress. Cover with thin plastic to prevent them drying.

8. Cut out six 40 mm scalloped circles to form the skirts and frill each circle with an anger tool. When the bodies of the dancers are dry, attach the bodices and skirts with egg white. Add a little bow of pink modelling paste to the front of each dress.

9. Pipe pale blue piping jelly onto the cake to form the pond and mould the rocks from brown modelling paste.

10. Make the arum lilies and leaves, following the steps in the photograph and position them around the pond, attaching them with royal icing.

11. Make the water lilies as shown and position them on the pond.

12. Mould blue bell-shaped flowers, following the instructions for hyacinths on page 40.

13. Roll out white modelling paste and cut out the daisies with a small daisy cutter. Mark the lines on each petal with a pin. Bend over the end of a piece of covered wire and then bend the hook over sideways. Thread the straight end through the centre of the daisy. Roll a tiny piece of yellow modelling paste into a ball and

press it against some net to mark it. Attach it to the centre of the daisy over the bent wire with a little egg white.

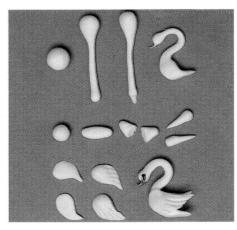

14. Mould two swans from white modelling paste as shown and when dry, paint the beaks and eyes with food colouring and a fine paintbrush. Position the swans on the pond.

15. Make forget-me-nots, in assorted pastel shades, and leaves from modelling paste and when dry, attach them to the top and at the base of the cake together with the candles.

16. Pipe tufts of grass where the dancers will stand, with green royal icing in a grass tube (Ateco 233). Position each dancer on a tuft of grass and support them with cocktail sticks until the royal icing has set.

17. Cut out a rectangle of white modelling paste and allow it to dry. Pipe on 'Happy birthday' and the child's name in white royal icing in a No. 2 writing tube. Pipe over this lettering with green royal icing in a No. 1 writing tube. Edge the plaque with a tiny shell border in white royal icing in a No. 1 writing tube.

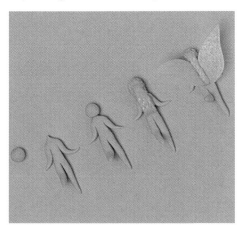

18. If you decide to make fairies, use the pattern on page 163 and cut out the wings from rice paper. Pipe the fairies' hair in yellow royal icing with a No. 1 writing tube and attach the wings as shown.

Faerie Glen

Rainbow-coloured plastic icing, fairies and toadstools combine to create this delightful fantasy cake.

INGREDIENTS

1 x 250 mm square cake (page 12)
250 g each of pale pink, blue, lemon and green plastic icing (page 14)
flesh-coloured, yellow and light brown royal icing (page 14)
green, lemon-yellow, orange and white modelling paste (page 14)

MATERIALS AND DECORATIONS

1 x 300 mm square cake board
Patterns for fairies (page 163), leaves (page 158)
brown and red food colouring
fine paintbrush
orange brush-on powder
forget-me-nots (page 40)
tube No. 1
small brush

1. Roll each colour of plastic icing into a sausage and place them next to each other. Fold them in half and then in half again four times in all.

2. Roll out the plastic icing and cover the cake.

3. Trace the fairy pictures onto the cake or onto waxed paper and outline and flood the fairies with flesh-coloured royal icing, following the instructions for Floodwork on page 31.

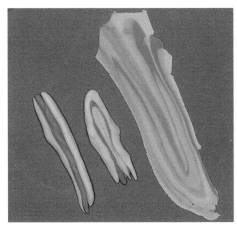

4. Colour modelling paste in assorted shades of green, lemon, orange and so on, and roll small portions of each colour into sausages. Lay the colours side by side then fold them in half, then in half again. Roll out this autumn-coloured paste and cut out a variety of leaves.

5. Shape the stems of the toadstools from modelling paste, cut them in half lengthwise and attach them to the top and sides of the cake with royal icing.

6. Using your fingers, shape orange and yellow modelling paste into mushroom caps, then cut them in half and attach them to the stems on the cake.

7. Following the picture, attach the leaves to the top and sides of the cake with royal icing.

8. Paint the features onto the faces of the fairies with food colouring and a fine paintbrush.

9. Roll out white modelling paste and cut out the wings. Dust the tips with orange brush-on powder and then attach the wings to the cake next to the fairies.

10. Cut out the skirts and the forget-me-nots from white modelling paste. Pipe tiny yellow royal icing dots into the centre of each flower. Attach the skirts and flowers to the fairies with royal icing.

11. Pipe on the hair with light brown royal icing in a No. 1 writing tube. Use a small brush to create the waves on the hair.

Egg~stra Special Eggs

Create your own delightful egg characters from commercial sugar eggs, modelling paste and food colouring.

RACING BUNNY

INGREDIENTS
pale blue pastillage (page 15)
rolling pin
scalloped oval cutter
white sugar egg
royal icing (page 14)
black, pale blue, yellow, brown and white
modelling paste (page 14)
snail's trail (page 21)
tubes Nos. 1 or 2
stamens

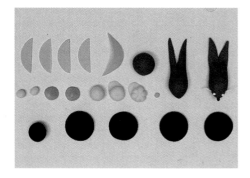

1. Roll out pale blue pastillage and cut out a scalloped oval. Allow it to dry.

2. Attach the egg horizontally to the pastillage plaque with royal icing and allow it to dry.

3. Flatten four balls (each smaller than a marble) of black modelling paste to form the wheels and attach them to the egg with royal icing.

4. Roll out pale blue modelling paste and cut out the windscreen and four mudguards. Set them aside to dry.

5. Make two headlamps from pale blue modelling paste and add yellow modelling paste for the lights. Attach to the egg.

6. Pipe a snail's trail with royal icing in a No. 1 or 2 writing tube along the windscreen and mudguards and add a dot of icing to the centre of each wheel.

7. Make the bunny's head from brown modelling paste, following the steps in the photograph. Pipe on the eyes and teeth with royal icing in a small writing tube or mould them in white modelling paste. Add short lengths of stamens for whiskers.

8. Mould the cap from a ball of yellow modelling paste and add a small ball of blue paste to the top.

9. Cut a strip from yellow modelling paste for the scarf and attach it, together with the head and cap, to the egg.

LORD AND LADY DUCK

INGREDIENTS
blue and pink pastillage (page 15)
rolling pin
2 x white sugar eggs
royal icing (page 14)
white, yellow, blue, black, pink, purple
and green modelling paste (page 14)
black food colouring
fine paintbrush
anger tool

1. Roll out blue and pink pastillage and cut out a scalloped circle from each colour. Allow them to dry thoroughly.

2. Attach the eggs horizontally to the plaques with royal icing and allow them to dry thoroughly.

3. Shape each tail from a small ball of white modelling paste and attach them with water to the narrow part of each egg.

4. Roll two balls of white modelling paste for the heads and attach them to the eggs.

5. Mould the wings from white modelling paste and attach them to the eggs.

6. Mould the beaks from yellow modelling paste as shown, fold them in half and secure them to the head with water.

7. Mould the feet from yellow modelling paste and stick them to the plaque.

8. Paint on the eyes with black food colouring and a fine paintbrush.

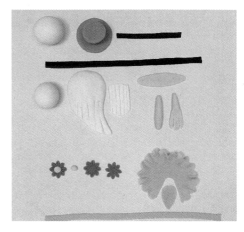

9. For *Lord Duck*, mould the top hat from blue modelling paste and add a strip of black paste for the band. Make a bow tie from a strip of black modelling paste and attach it, together with the top hat, to the gentleman bird.

10. For *Lady Duck*, roll out pink modelling paste and cut out the bonnet and bow. Frill the edges of the bonnet with an anger tool and attach the bonnet and bow to the lady bird. Cut out the flowers with a tiny flower cutter, and two leaves, and attach them to the plaque with a little royal icing.

EASTER EGG

INGREDIENTS
pale blue pastillage (page 15)
rolling pin
cookie cutter
white sugar egg
royal icing (page 14)
green and pale blue modelling paste
    (page 14)
blue ribbon

1. Roll out pale blue pastillage, cut out a scalloped circle or oval and allow to dry.

2. Attach the egg horizontally to the plaque with royal icing.

3. Cut out tiny leaves and flowers, adding a dot of royal icing to the centre of each flower.

4. Attach the blue ribbon to the egg, add a bow and attach the flowers and leaves with royal icing.

HAPPY CLOWN

INGREDIENTS
pale green pastillage (page 15)
rolling pin
cookie cutter
egg white
royal icing (page 14)
coloured sugar crystals
white sugar egg
black food colouring
fine paintbrush
green, orange, red and yellow modelling
    paste (page 14)
piece of thin plastic
scissors
pink brush-on powder

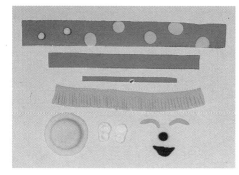

1. Roll out pale green pastillage and cut out a scalloped circle with a cookie cutter. Brush with egg white or thin royal icing and sprinkle on coloured sugar crystals leaving a 10 mm circle clear in the centre. Allow it to dry thoroughly.

2. Attach the egg, narrow part downwards, to the pastillage plaque with royal icing and allow it to dry thoroughly.

3. Paint eyes on the egg with black food colouring and a fine paintbrush.

4. Roll out green modelling paste and cut out the three strips as shown, covering them with thin plastic to prevent them drying out. Attach one strip around the neck to form a collar.

5. Roll out orange modelling paste and cut out a rectangle for the hair. Cut the strip with a pair of scissors to create a fringe effect and attach it to the egg with royal icing.

6. Mould red modelling paste to form a mouth and nose and tiny pieces of orange paste into eyebrows and attach them to the face.

7. Mould the hat from yellow modelling paste, add the small green strip for the band and attach the hat to the egg with royal icing.

8. Place small balls of yellow paste onto the large green strip, flattening them by rolling over them with a rolling pin. Fold the strip into a bow and attach it to the clown with a little water.

9. Brush the clown's cheeks with a little pink brush-on powder.

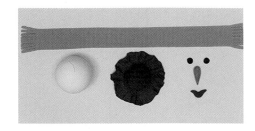

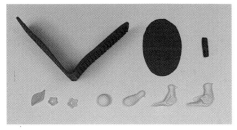

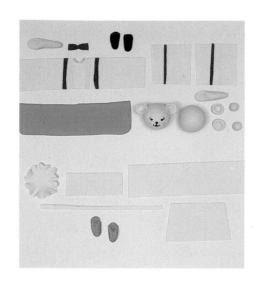

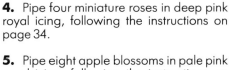

In Miniature

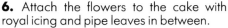

These enchanting miniatures require as much skill as do full-sized cakes.

RECTANGULAR CAKE

A miniature cake to celebrate that special occasion.

INGREDIENTS
1 x 110 x 75 x 50 mm deep cake (page 12)
250 g white plastic icing (page 14)
pale green, dark and pale pink and
    yellow royal icing (page 14)

MATERIALS AND DECORATIONS
1 x 120 x 85 mm cake board
tiny half-round crimper
tubes Nos. 0 or 1, 87 (Ateco)
piped roses (page 34)
piped apple blossoms and leaves
    (page 32)

1. Cover the cake with white plastic icing and immediately crimp around the top edge with a tiny half-round crimper.

2. Pipe a border around the base of the cake with green royal icing in a No. 87 Ateco fancy border tube.

3. Overline the crimping with pale green royal icing in a No. 0 or 1 writing tube.

4. Pipe four miniature roses in deep pink royal icing, following the instructions on page 34.

5. Pipe eight apple blossoms in pale pink royal icing, following the instructions on page 32. Pipe a dot of yellow royal icing into the centre of each flower.

6. Attach the flowers to the cake with royal icing and pipe leaves in between.

WEDDING CAKE

For the sentimental, a miniature replica can be made of the actual wedding cake. Extension work, loops and moulded flowers are used to create this attractive memento.

INGREDIENTS

1 x 75 mm round cake (page 12)
1 x 125 mm round cake
500 g white plastic icing (page 14)
white royal icing (page 14)
white and mauve modelling paste
    (page 14)

MATERIALS AND DECORATIONS

1 x 100 mm round cake board
1 x 170 mm round cake board
tubes Nos. 0, 00, 1, 2
snail's trail (page 21)
pattern for miniature orchids (page 158)
fine covered florist wire
mauve brush-on powder
ball tool
florist tape
miniature white ribbon bows
50 x 40 mm high acrylic stand

1. Cover both cakes with plastic icing.

2. Pipe the embroidery design with white royal icing in a No. 0 or 00 writing tube. The design is piped directly onto the cakes as described on page 24.

3. Pipe a snail's trail around the lower edge of each cake with a No. 1 or 2 writing tube.

4. Execute the extension work by following the instructions on page 26.

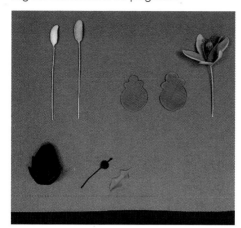

5. Mould eight tiny orchids by rolling small pieces of white modelling paste into elongated shapes to form the centres and attaching these to pieces of fine covered wire. Curve the centres slightly and set them aside to dry thoroughly. Brush them with mauve brush-on powder.

6. Cut out the orchid trumpets from mauve modelling paste and flute around the scalloped part. Wet the base of each trumpet before attaching it to the centre.

7. Cut out five-petal shapes (page 158), hollow each petal slightly with a ball tool, wet the centre and slip the wire attached to the trumpet through the centre. Set the orchids aside to dry, then tape them together to form two sprays.

8. Pipe a row of dots all along the top edge of the extension work and then pipe the loops using a No. 0 or 00 writing tube.

9. Attach the flower sprays and ribbon bows to the cakes. Position the stand on the bottom tier and place the other tier on top.

CHRISTMAS CAKE

An ideal gift for that special someone living on their own.

INGREDIENTS

1 x 110 x 75 x 50 mm deep cake (page 12)
250 g white plastic icing (page 14)
red, brown, green and white modelling
    paste (page 14)
pale green and white royal icing
    (page 14)

MATERIALS AND DECORATIONS

1 x 120 x 85 mm cake board
ribbed roller
straight-edge cutter
cotton wool
pair of scissors
pattern for holly leaves (page 158)
black stamens
tubes Nos. 0, 5
shell border (page 22)

1. Cover the cake with white plastic icing.

2. Roll out a strip of red modelling paste and then roll over it with a ribbed roller. Cut 10 mm wide ribbons with a straight-edge cutter. Attach the ribbons to the cake with a little water or royal icing.

3. Form two loops with strips of red paste, supporting them with cotton wool to hold their shape until they are dry.

4. Roll three small pieces of brown modelling paste into egg shapes and snip small sections with a pair of scissors to form the pine cones.

5. Roll out green modelling paste and cut out several holly leaves.

6. Form holly berries by rolling red modelling paste into small balls and inserting a black stamen into each one.

7. Roll out white modelling paste and cut out a small rectangle for the tag. Pipe on the lettering and edge the tag with small dots with pale green royal icing in a No. 0 writing tube.

8. Attach the ribbon loops, cones and holly leaves and berries to the cake.

9. Pipe a small shell border around the base of the cake with white royal icing in a No. 5 star tube.

Part Three

Patterns

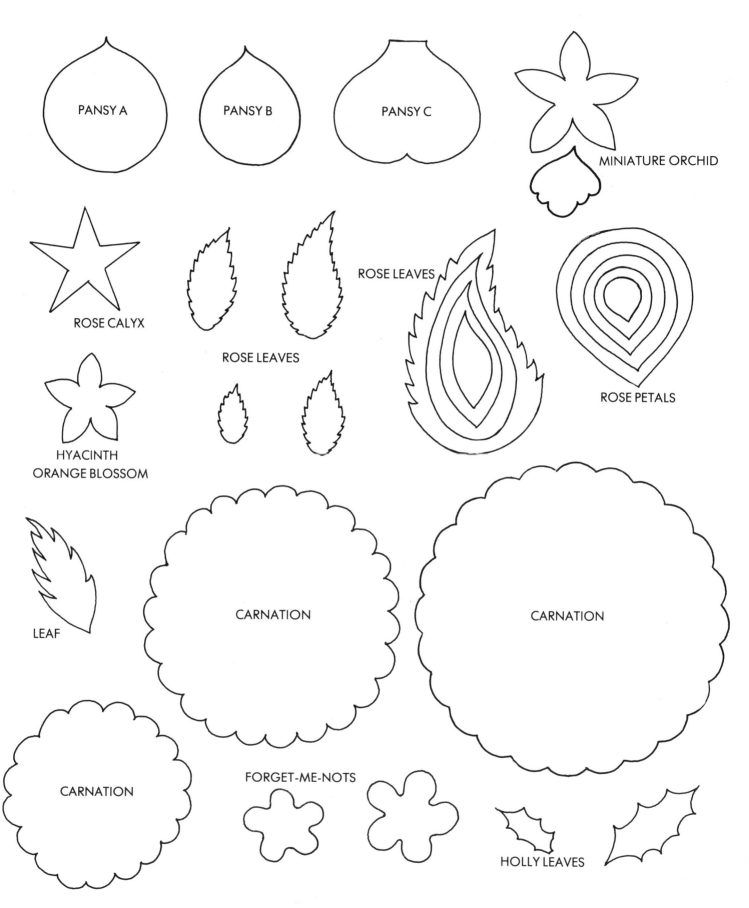

PANSY A

PANSY B

PANSY C

MINIATURE ORCHID

ROSE CALYX

ROSE LEAVES

ROSE LEAVES

ROSE PETALS

HYACINTH
ORANGE BLOSSOM

LEAF

CARNATION

CARNATION

CARNATION

FORGET-ME-NOTS

HOLLY LEAVES

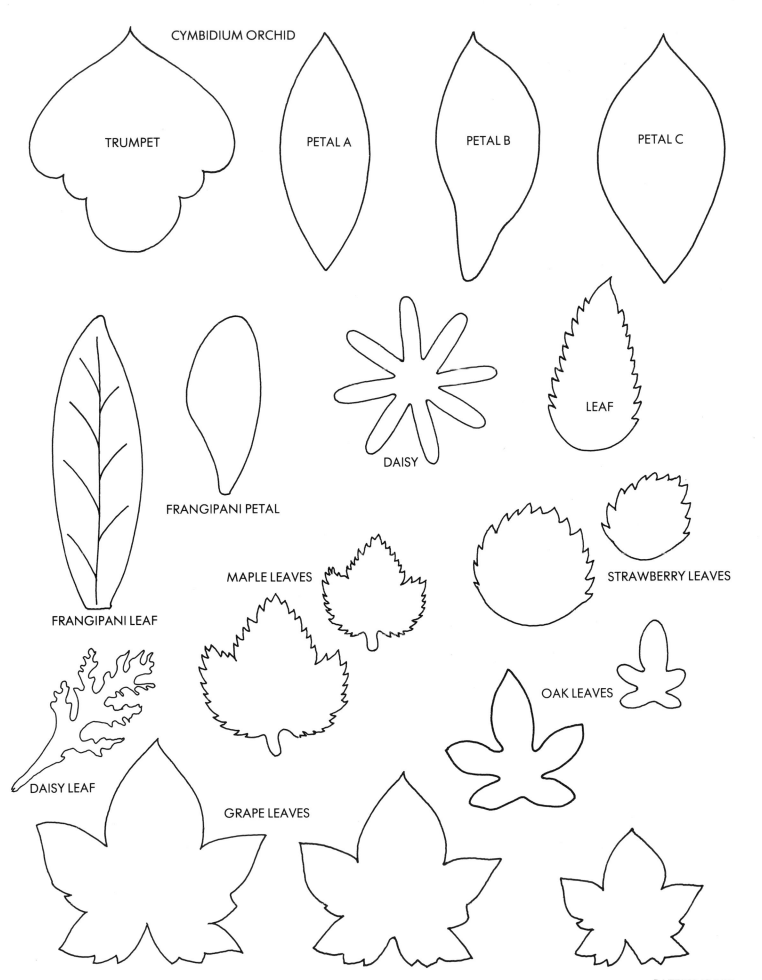

CYMBIDIUM ORCHID

TRUMPET

PETAL A

PETAL B

PETAL C

FRANGIPANI PETAL

DAISY

LEAF

FRANGIPANI LEAF

MAPLE LEAVES

STRAWBERRY LEAVES

OAK LEAVES

DAISY LEAF

GRAPE LEAVES

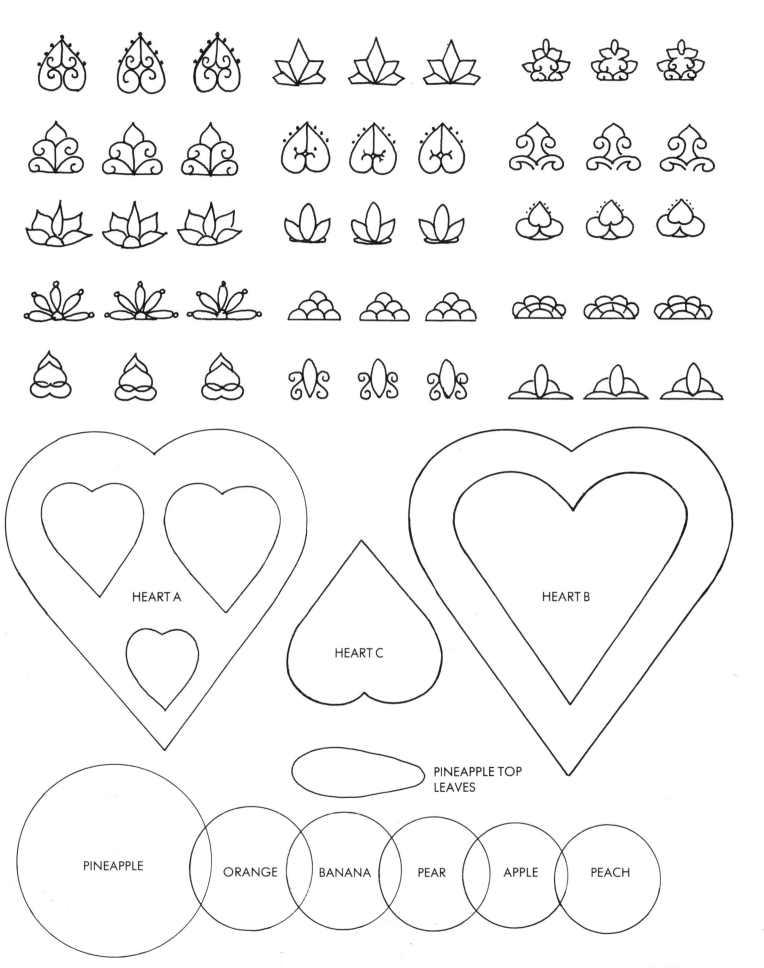

HEART A

HEART B

HEART C

PINEAPPLE TOP
LEAVES

PINEAPPLE

ORANGE

BANANA

PEAR

APPLE

PEACH

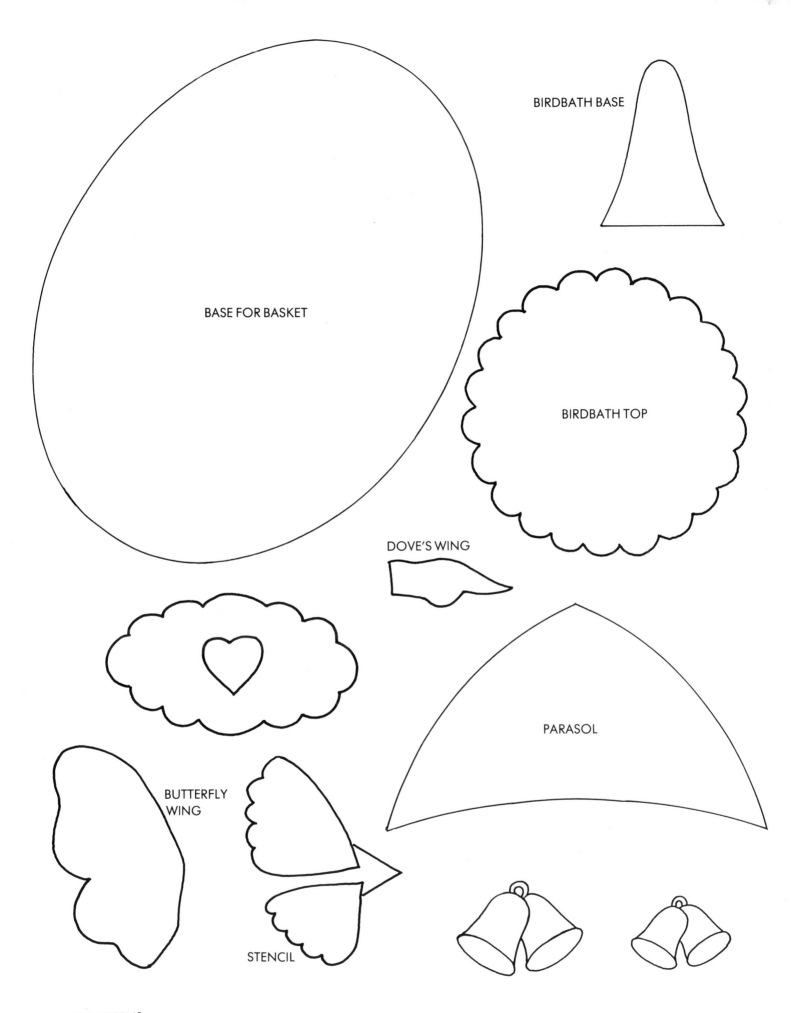

BIRDBATH BASE

BASE FOR BASKET

BIRDBATH TOP

DOVE'S WING

PARASOL

BUTTERFLY
WING

STENCIL

FAIRY WING

GRANNY

MY FAMILY TREE

NANA

MARY BORN 24/12/84

MOM

DAD

GRANDPA

MY BROTHER

MY SISTER

PAPA

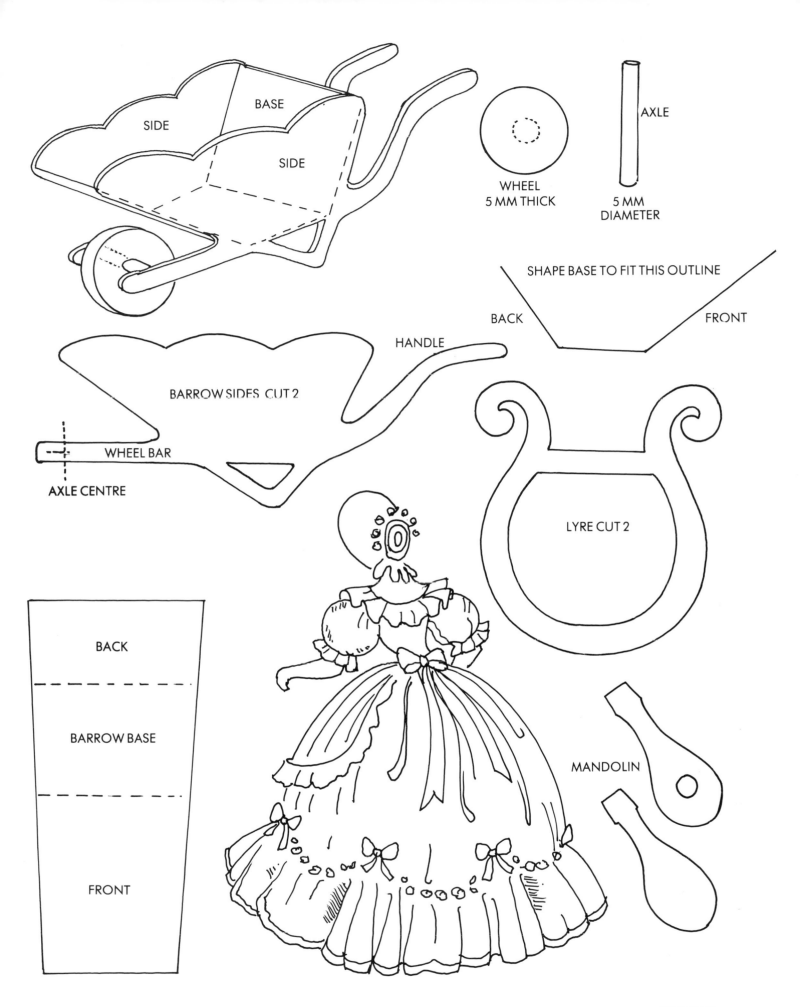

BASE

SIDE

SIDE

WHEEL
5 MM THICK

AXLE

5 MM
DIAMETER

SHAPE BASE TO FIT THIS OUTLINE

BACK

FRONT

HANDLE

BARROW SIDES CUT 2

WHEEL BAR

AXLE CENTRE

LYRE CUT 2

BACK

BARROW BASE

FRONT

MANDOLIN

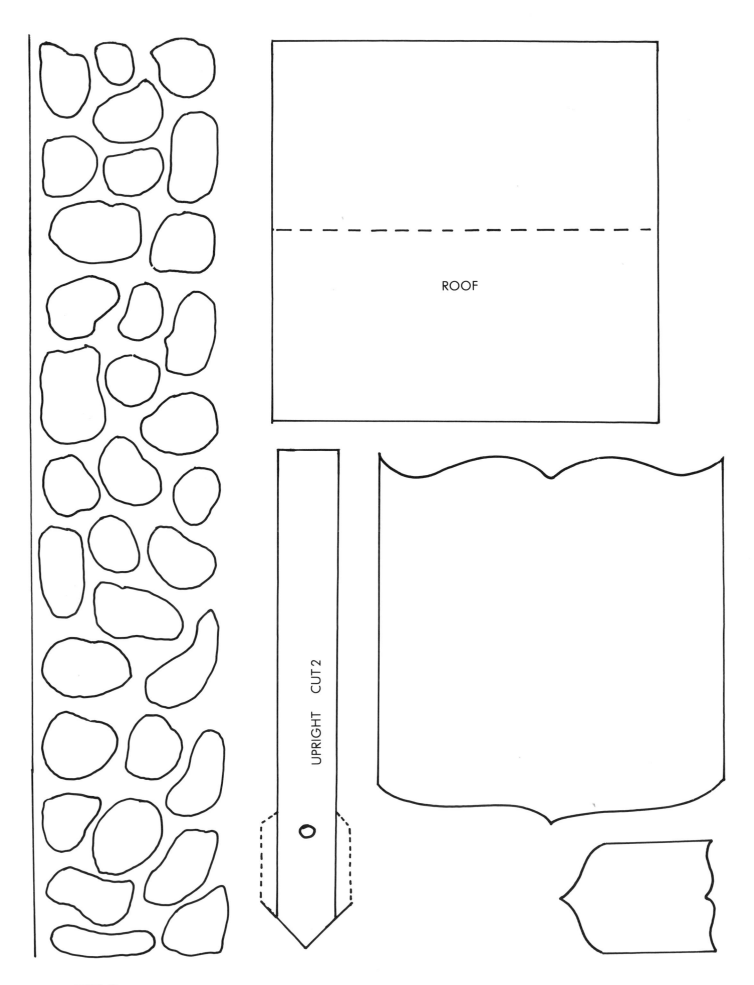

ROOF

UPRIGHT   CUT 2

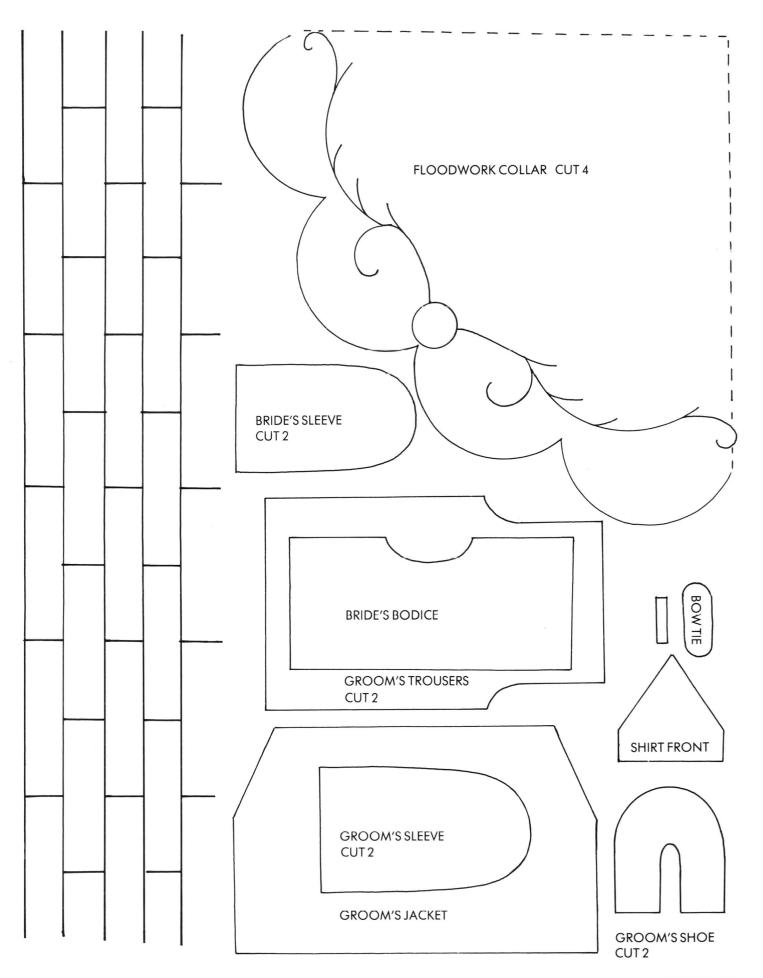

FLOODWORK COLLAR   CUT 4

BRIDE'S SLEEVE
CUT 2

BRIDE'S BODICE

GROOM'S TROUSERS
CUT 2

BOW TIE

SHIRT FRONT

GROOM'S SLEEVE
CUT 2

GROOM'S JACKET

GROOM'S SHOE
CUT 2

PENNANT

HULL

SAIL 3

SAIL 1

SAIL 4

SAIL 2

SPINNAKER

FOOT OF CRADLE

BASE OF CRADLE

HEADBOARD
OF CRADLE

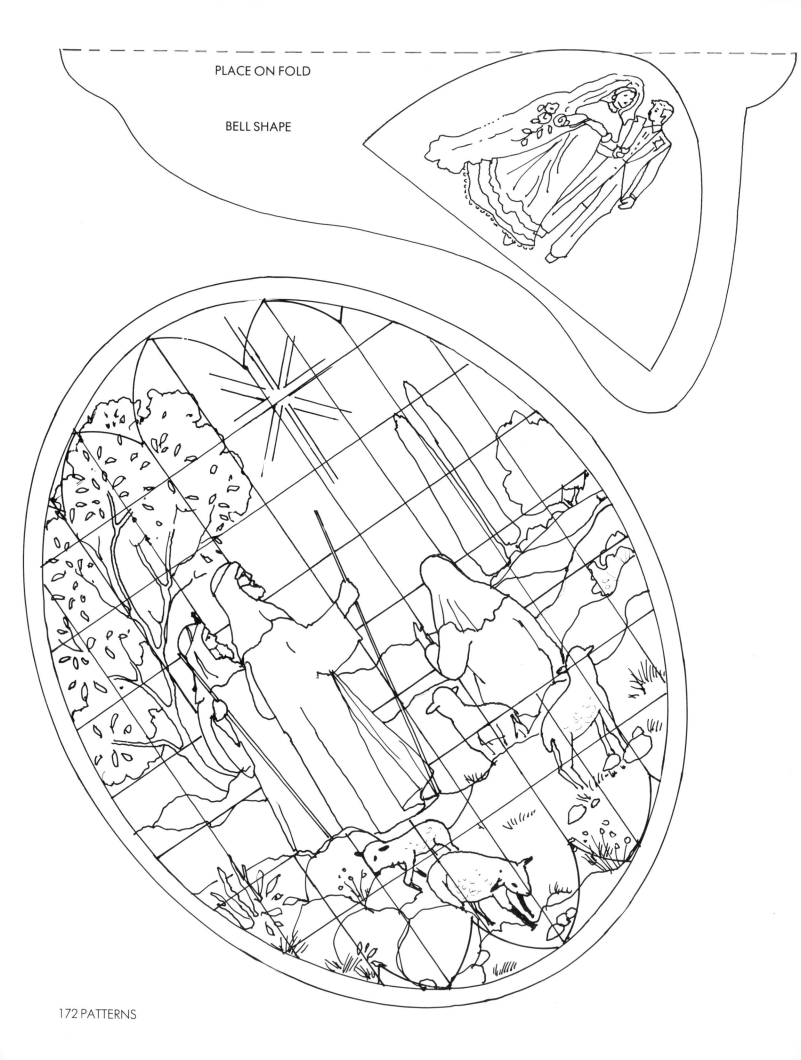

PLACE ON FOLD

BELL SHAPE

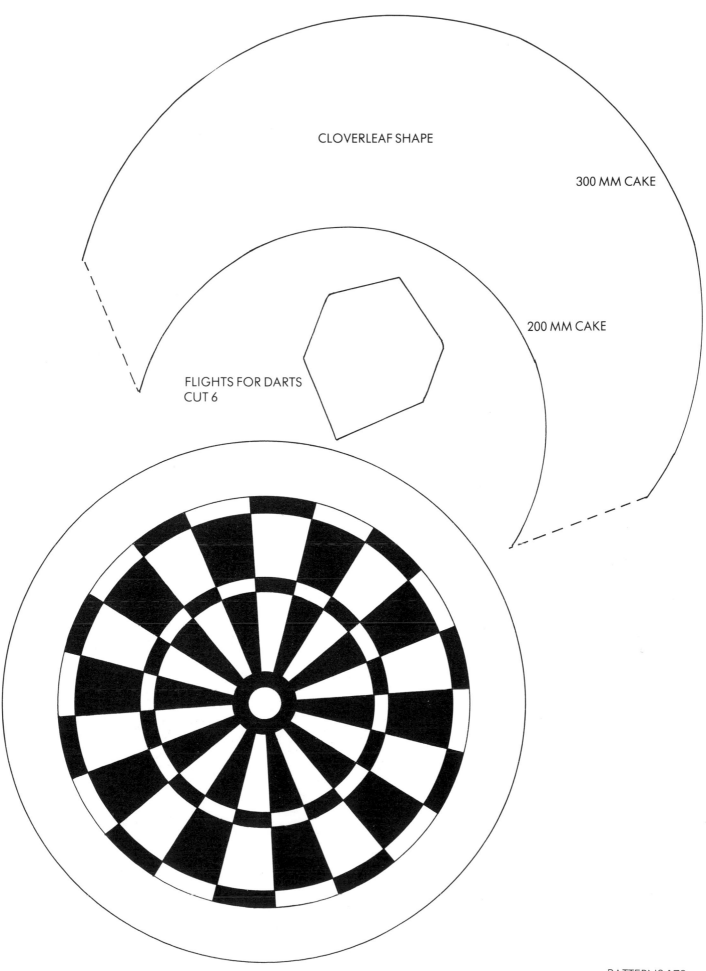

CLOVERLEAF SHAPE

300 MM CAKE

200 MM CAKE

FLIGHTS FOR DARTS
CUT 6

abcdefghijkl
mnopqrstuv
wxyz ABCDE
FGHIJKLMNO
PQRSTUVW
XYZ 12345678
90 ABCDEFGH
IJKLMNOPQ
RSTUVWXY
Zabcdefghijklmnopqrstuv
wxyz 1234567890 &

16 21 25

21 21

TODAY

ABC MOTHER

1234567890

ABCDEFGHIJKLMNOPQ

RSTUVWXYZ

1234567890 50

INDEX